# Using stories

# RE and Citizenship

Ages 7-9

Sam Densham

HOPSCOTCH EDUCATIONAL PUBLISHING

Sam Densham started out working as an actress in theatre in education, where she also taught, directed and wrote scripts. After having a baby in 1997 she took a break from theatre and started a teaching career specialising in drama and PSHE. She now runs her own business both teaching drama and communication skills and entertaining.

Published by Hopscotch Educational Publishing Ltd,
Unit 2, The Old Brushworks, 56 Pickwick Road,
Corsham, Wilts SN13 9BX
Tel: 01249 701701

© 2005 Hopscotch Educational Publishing

Written by Sam Densham
Series design by Blade Communications
Illustrated by Robin Lawrie
Cover illustration by Pat Murray
Printed by Cle-print

Sam Densham hereby asserts her moral right to be identified as the author of this work in accordance with the Copyright, Designs and Patents Act, 1988.

ISBN 1-904307-97-3

# Contents

# Introduction

## Why citizenship?

In a democratic, multicultural society it is important for children to grow up with a grasp of what it means to be a good citizen, so that they can play a conscious part in making their local and wider community a better place for everyone. In a society like ours, in which political issues are complex and decisions are made by professional politicians, many young people feel that society gives them little and that they owe it nothing. By teaching citizenship at primary level we can help children to understand that they do have an important and rewarding role to play and that they have an effect on everyone with whom they come into contact.

## Why religious stories?

A religion is often confused with its outward appearances. It is possible to teach children about rites of passage and the historical origins of religions without them really understanding the philosophy of the religion. The stories of the religions, on the other hand, contain the essence of the religion. Moreover, they show how this essence is played out in a social context.

There are other good reasons for teaching citizenship through religious stories. Stories in themselves are an excellent teaching medium – a fact recognised by many religions. Children identify with the characters and become absorbed in the story. On the simplest level, they want to know what happens next. But when the story is over, there are always questions to ask. All the stories in this book raise questions relating to ethics and citizenship. They encourage children to discuss personal and social issues and to become aware of the choices they have to make as citizens.

## The multicultural aspect

Children in our schools come from a wide variety of ethnic and religious backgrounds. Even those from families with no particular religious belief are influenced by their peers and by the largely Judaeo-Christian basis of our society's legal code. The stories in this book are taken from nine different spiritual traditions. They illustrate a wide variety of lifestyles, from all over the world and from different eras. They collectively embody a wisdom whose value is shown by the longevity of the stories and by their shared themes and messages. The stories will help teach children the universality of human concerns, encouraging tolerance and appreciation of other cultures and ethnic groups. We live in a society which is hugely diverse, yet our similarities are at least as strong as our differences.

## The structure of the book

Each section is based on a single story. There are two stories for each of the six most widespread spiritual traditions and one story for each of three less well known traditions. Each section begins with teachers' notes. These include:

❑ a short introduction suggesting the number of lessons over which to spread the section, and one or two other stories in the book to which it relates;

❑ the main themes of the story;

❑ related Citizenship units;

❑ aims of the lesson;

❑ resources needed (typically, copies of the story and a worksheet);

❑ background: the source of the story and how the story reflects the religion;

❑ whole class starter: an activity to engage children in the issues raised by the story, particularly those relating to citizenship, before reading the story;

❑ activities for you to choose from;

❑ plenary: rounding off the lesson;

❑ differentiation: ideas;

❑ extension activities.

## How to use the book

We suggest that you do the Starter activity with the class in order to get them thinking about the issues in the story, and relating these issues to their own lives. Then read the story aloud, with the children following it in their copies. You will usually find that the children want to comment on the story and discuss it, so encourage this before settling them down to the activities suggested. You could introduce information from the Background section at this point.

Note that a choice of main activities is provided. The easier ones tend to come first, but there are also separate suggestions for differentiation. You could have the whole class working on a single activity, but in many cases it would be possible for groups of children to work on different activities. However, you should all come together for the plenary. After all, citizenship is about a shared experience, and sharing what has been learned is an exercise in citizenship in itself!

## The stories

The stories have been retold for this book but their key elements are based closely on original sources. Sometimes different versions of a story are available, in which case the retelling usually merges aspects of these different versions.

The stories take many forms. Some are about the founders of religions or about other significant figures, such as 'Siddhartha and the swan', which shows Siddhartha, the founder of the Buddhist religion, as a child showing compassion to animals. This compassion theme is reflected in the Native American story of 'The wind, the rain and the sparrow', but this story is purely folklore handed down from family to family with no basis in history.

All of the stories are designed to be a starting point from which to develop citizenship within the classroom, and have a lot of potential to motivate thought and discussion about many of the units in the Citizenship Scheme of Work.

Some of the stories, such as 'The good Samaritan', are already quite well known and are used in our society to teach a lesson (as was originally intended). The stories expand on basic themes. For example, the Sikh story of 'The emperor and the Langar' explores the nature of community; another story, 'The river goddess', looks at our effect on the environment, encouraging children to see the need for individual responsibility. All the stories and activities are written to stimulate and enthuse children, allowing them to absorb the social and personal messages contained in the Citizenship Units.

# CHAPTER 1

# Respect for our world – Animism

This chapter is based on a story from the Animist religion called 'The river goddess'. The story tells of what can happen to our environment if we take it for granted. It asks children to consider the implications of our actions, and would link well with the story of 'The wind, the rain and the sparrow' (see Chapter 13). There are also extension activities for children to look at ideas for developing school grounds.

## Themes

Respect, awareness and understanding of our effect on the environment.

## Citizenship Scheme of Work

Unit 5 – Living in a diverse world
Unit 6 – Developing our school grounds

## Aims

• To develop an understanding of the world around us and how we have an effect on it.
• To look at how other cultures view the world.
• To see how we need to look after our world so it can look after us.

## Resources

• The story on page 8
• The photocopiable sheets on pages 10 and 11

## About this religion

Many people think that Animism is the oldest form of religion. The essence of its belief is that everything, living or not living, has a soul. Because of this Animists worship many different things, such as plants and rivers. Some have even worshipped the cocoa tree!

## Whole class starter

❑ Tell the children about Animism, then ask them to look around the classroom at all the objects and choose one that they think an Animist would worship. It could be a rubber because it helps them to get rid of their mistakes, or a pen because it helps them write down and keep their thoughts, or the door because it keeps out the draught.

❑ Once the children have chosen their object ask them to draw it and write a few words about why an Animist might want to worship it. Collect the ideas together and, as a class, discuss each other's opinions.

❑ Now read the story.

## Activities

❑ Ask the children the following questions:

• What would have happened to the village if it had not rained?

• What was the village doing to its environment? Can you see any similarities with our world today?

• The people made a sacrifice to save their village. Is there something that people can do, like a sacrifice, to save our environment? (Suggest not driving cars, walking to school or switching off the lights in empty rooms).

□ Using copies of the questionnaire on page 10, ask the children to collect data from other people in the school so that they can make a plan of action on helping our environment. Once they have gathered all the information, plot it on a bar chart to see if there is a pattern that may help to decide on a plan of action. Discuss the data and ask the children what could happen next.

□ Ask the children what they know about climate. Discuss the weather conditions in our country and the types of crops we can grow. Extend this to climates in other parts of the world. Give the children copies of the climate pictures (page 11) and ask them which pictures show dry climates, cold climates, wet ones and so on. Once they have sorted through the pictures, ask the children where they would choose to live. Ask them to draw their favourite place with an explanation of what they like about it, and why they would want to live there.

## Differentiation
□ More able children can draw and describe the part of the world they like least, adding the type of work that they might have to do there.

□ Less able children can copy the words 'I would like living here because' and then add their own words to the sentence.

## Extension activities
□ Set up a committee to look at how the school and grounds could be developed in an environmentally friendly way. Suggest avoiding concrete, using wood from replenishable sources and water- and power-saving measures. Develop a policy to use throughout the school.

□ In groups, ask the children to list the positive and negative points of each climate picture.

□ Ask the children to write a story or poem about what could happen to either the school or the world if we don't look after it. Ask if they think school will be a nice place to be in if nobody picks up their litter, or the world, if we keep cutting down the trees. Suggest the following starters:

- 'If I had cared for my school the football pitch would still be there and…'

- 'Look at the world now, no grass to be seen…'

- 'No more trees, no more green…'

- 'When I was young I could eat the snow, but now…'

## Plenary session
□ Ask the children why the river in the story dried up. Explain that the goddess held back the rain because she saw that the people of Osogbo were taking the land for granted and they needed to be stopped. Ask the children to compare what happened in the story to the state of our planet now – can they think of any areas of the world that are under threat? (For example, rainforests being cut down and ice caps melting.) What about closer to home? Are there any disused canals or playing fields? Is there anything that the children can do to prevent these things from happening or getting worse?

# The river goddess

The river meanders through the jungle, waves lapping at its shore, children splashing and laughing. Then the procession begins. The people of Osogbo bring grain and offerings of garlands made from brightly coloured blossom or feathers in many shapes and sizes, some shaped like the wings of the birds that circle above. They are waiting.

The children stop playing and the villagers stop talking as the king of the village offers prayers. He throws a handful of grain into the air and watches it rain down onto the surface of the water bringing the river to life. Immediately the birds swoop down from the sky, children splash and all the garlands and offerings follow as the waves rise up to collect them. The foam washes the bank as the current gathers speed. The villagers cheer and begin to sing – a magnificent end to a long day.

'Mummy,' says a little girl, as her mother wipes droplets of water from her face, 'why do we throw grain at the river?'

'We don't throw it at her! We give it to her, to say thank you!' her mother replies.

'But why do we need to say thank you? What does the river do?' asks the little girl.

'Without the river we would all die! Do you know that the river is called Osun?'

'Yes, of course I know that.'

'Well, have you heard the story of Osun?'

The little girl shakes her head.

Osun was once a beautiful woman, but she turned herself into water to become a goddess.'

'So the river is a goddess?' asks the child.

'Yes. A long time ago our village was much smaller. But living by such a beautiful river here amongst the trees, our village became successful and began to grow. More and more strong babies were born. More crops were grown on the land to feed our cattle, more fish were taken from the river and more water was used from Osun. The villagers were happy and prosperous and everyone assumed it would always be so, no matter how much was taken.'

'Did the king give Osun his grain in those days?' asks the child.

'No. No one even thought about Osun and the work she did. She was taken for granted. Everyone believed she would always be there. That is why when the river began to dry up it was a shock. The crops began to die. Cattle became weak and feeble and children fell ill. King Laro realised that there had been no rain to fill the river for months. Soon Osun was no more than a muddy trickle of water.

'Anxiously, the king spoke to the wise elders of the village. They said that the goddess Osun must be angry and the king must find out why.

'So early one morning the king went alone to the banks of the river to ask what was making her so angry. He waited and waited, getting hotter and thirstier, until at last, as he bent his head to sip water from the muddy river-bottom, he felt warmth fill his body, spreading from his lips to his toes, and he heard a soft voice talking to him.

'"Your village has taken from me year after year, never giving anything in return. You must show your gratitude. You must learn to give. Trust in me and do as I ask, and then I will look after your people again."

'The goddess told King Laro to take all that was left in the village and throw it to her. They must sacrifice all the grain and all the animals that had survived the drought, to show that they would change.

'King Laro walked back to the village in silence, except for the distant rustling of dry leaves. Once there he set about his tasks, and no one dared question the king, although some were afraid because they were losing the last of their food.

'As the king threw everything down onto the river bed there were tears in his eyes. As the last of the grain fell into the muddy sludge a loud crash of thunder was heard in the distance.

'The people waited. The sky grew dark as clouds formed above the trees and then, with an even louder crash, a cascade of water stormed along the course of the river, chasing along the dusty dry banks. The villagers cheered and danced in the rain – which didn't stop for three days!'

'And did everyone in the village survive, Mummy?' asks the little girl, wiping a raindrop from her nose.

'Oh, yes my dear! And to celebrate and give thanks, King Laro decreed that we give sacrifice to Osun at this time every year, so that we will never take the river goddess for granted again.'

Name _____

# Recycling

All these things can be sent for recycling.
Find out what people think should be recycled at your school.
Put one tick by each thing that they think should be recycled.

glass

plastic

paper

cans

printer cartridges

old mobile phones

old clothes

Who will be in charge of recycling?
Ask people for their ideas and write them here.

Where will you collect the things to be recycled? What will you put them in?
Ask people for their ideas and write them here.

PHOTOCOPIABLE

# Different climates

# CHAPTER 2

# Helping others – Buddhism

This chapter is based on a Buddhist story called the 'Thousand–armed Chenrezig'. The Thousand–armed Chenrezig devotes his life to helping humanity overcome its suffering. It links well to Units 1 and 4 of the Citizenship SoW. The story would work well alongside the Jewish story 'The greatest gift of all' (see Chapter 11) which also looks at compassion and communication.

## Themes

Self discipline, focus, communication

## Citizenship Scheme of Work

Unit 1 – Taking part – developing skills of communication and participation
Unit 4 – People who help us

## Aims

- To learn how to listen and communicate effectively and to think about how important it is to care for others.
- To recognise conflicting views and learn how to respond with ideas for solutions.
- To learn that being dedicated and focused will help to achieve a goal.

## Resources

- The story on page 14
- The photocopiable sheets on pages 16 and 17

## About this religion

The religion of Buddhism takes for granted that suffering exists in the world but tries to eradicate it. It teaches that suffering will exist as long as people long for or want and desire things, whether they are material or emotional things. Buddha taught that there is no eternal god who is independent of the universe, and so the religion has many buddhas to help with personal spiritual development.

## Whole class starter

❏ Explain to the class that you are going to read them a story from the Buddhist religion. It is a story about a special person wanting to help everyone in the world.

❏ Explain that these words from Buddhism will also be used in the story:

*Mantra* – a special prayer that's repeated over and over again.
*Bodhisattva* – a living being who devotes their life to becoming enlightened and saving others from suffering. (Ask what the children think is meant by suffering. Is it something like toothache or a bruised knee, or something different?)

❏ Now read the story.

## Activities

❏ Ask the children the following questions:

- What did Avalokiteshvara vow to do?

- What sort of suffering was he talking about?

- What did he have on each hand? How could this help him to end suffering?

❏ Discuss how Chenrezig's arms could allow him to help more people; remember that each arm had an eye in the palm of the hand. Ask the children if they can think of something they could add to their bodies that would allow them to help others. Suggest examples like: with extra arms they could help their parents more around the house; with longer legs they could run faster and carry messages; an extra head could help you see both sides of an argument.

❑ Look at the picture of Chenrezig (page 16) and ask the children to draw a picture of themselves with something added. At the bottom of the picture they need to explain how the new body part will make it easier for them to help others.

❑ Remind the children that Avalokiteshvara had an ambition to help everyone in the world. Ask them to talk about their ambitions and dreams. Explain that to achieve anything in life you have to set your mind to it and work hard; even reading and writing only come with hard work and practice.

❑ Tell the children that they are each going to choose someone who they think achieved their ambition, and then on Activity sheet 2 (page 17) write down what makes this person a success. It might be a sportsperson or an entertainer or someone they know. Make it clear that this must be a real person, not a fictional character.

❑ Ask each child to make a list of things they will need to do to make their own ambitions come true.

## Differentiation

❑ More able children could turn their initial list into a letter to send to someone who has achieved their ambition. In the letter the children should say a little about themselves, explain why they think of this person as a hero and finally ask for a few tips on how to be successful.

❑ Less able children could use a letter template to help them construct a letter to send to their hero.

## Extension

❑ Give each child an individual challenge, for example: learning difficult spellings; learning a song to perform; counting to 10 in five different languages; a ball skills challenge, such as juggling; a handwriting challenge.

❑ Set challenges for groups from the class. Explain that the group has to aim to complete the challenge by a set date when you will judge whether or not they have been successful. Before you start, talk to the children about what they will need to do to successfully complete their challenges.

❑ Organise the children into pairs. Explain that one child from each pair is going to talk to their partner for two minutes. (Give them a topic such as the environment, a topical news event, or a class topic.) Tell them the importance of speaking clearly, and with enough volume. While the first child is talking, the other child has to stay completely silent, and at the end of the two minutes the listener has to recall at least three facts from the talk. If there is time swap around.

## Plenary session

❑ Remind the children that Chenrezig vowed to help everyone but, as dedicated as he was, he found it difficult. Ask the children to show some of their pictures with different parts added, and discuss the outcomes as if they were real – are some more helpful than others?

❑ Explain to the children that Chenrezig followed through on his vow. Even though, as Avalokiteshvara, he had a moment of doubt, his own suffering (of being split apart) gave him more strength, determination and understanding to be able to continue his work of helping others and he remained dedicated to his cause.

# Thousand-armed Chenrezig

This story is about somebody with a very difficult name – Avalokiteshvara. Can you say Avalokiteshvara?

Try and break it down – AV-AL-O-KIT-ESH-VA-RA.

To make matters worse, later on in this story Avalokiteshvara's name changes and he becomes known as 'Thousand-armed Chenrezig'. Wouldn't it be so much easier if he was called Bob? But then 'Thousand-armed Bob' doesn't have quite the same ring to it as 'Thousand-armed Chenrezig'! So why did Avalokiteshvara's name change to Chenrezig? And how did he get all those arms?

Well, Avalokiteshvara was a buddha. He lived a long time ago in a place called Tibet. He cared very much for all human beings and wanted to stop the suffering that he could see around him. So, in front of a thousand other buddhas and his religious teacher Amitabha, he vowed to spend his life working to end the suffering of human beings. And as if that wasn't enough, he added this: "May my head be cracked in ten and my body split into a thousand pieces if I ever even think about giving up my task."

You can probably guess what happens later on… that's right, he has a tiny doubt about his task. But why?

For many years Avalokiteshvara spent all his time meditating. He repeated a special mantra over and over, day after day, season after season, praying for the suffering in the world to come to an end. One day he stopped to have a look at the results of his work. Surely after all the years of meditation there must be hardly any suffering left, Avalokiteshvara thought.

But as he looked at the world around him he was shocked and disappointed to see that very little had changed. Yes, in some places there had been improvements; things were a little better; a few people were happier. But this was only a fraction of what he had hoped and wished for. There was still so much suffering all around the world, so much fighting, distrust and bitterness causing pain and sorrow.

PHOTOCOPIABLE

In that instant, as he looked around him and realised how little difference his work had made, he felt such despair that a moment of doubt clouded his mind. For just one fraction of a second he wanted to give up. His vow was broken and his terrible promise came true. First his head split into ten separate pieces, and then his body shattered into a thousand more. He screamed in agony and his teacher Amitabha heard him.

At once Amitabha was there. He took the pieces of Avalokiteshvara's body and joined them back together, but decided to give him a thousand arms, each one with an eye in its palm, so that he would be able to help many, many more people.

Finally Amitabha picked up the ten pieces of Avalokiteshvara's head. Instead of giving Avalokiteshvara one ordinary head he gave him eleven faces: nine compassionate ones, one wrathful and finally his own face at the top. Avalokiteshvara was remade as a new buddha. From now on he would be known as 'Thousand-armed Chenrezig'.

Chenrezig's only thoughts now were to free all living things from suffering. With his new form – a thousand arms to reach out to people, a thousand eyes to see suffering with, and eleven faces to understand and feel more – he was all the more able to give that help. Chenrezig had become a bodhisattva.

# Thousand-armed Chenrezig

ACTIVITY SHEET 1

PHOTOCOPIABLE

Name _____

# Achievement

Choose someone who has achieved their ambition. This might be someone famous or someone you know. Complete the chart below with details about this person.

Name of person _____

Details of the person:

_____

_____

_____

_____

_____

_____

Either draw a picture of the person or cut one out from a magazine or newspaper and stick it here.

I think this person achieved their ambition because _____

_____

_____

_____

_____

_____

_____

_____

# Caring for animals – Buddhism

Like 'Thousand-armed Chenrezig' in the previous section, this Buddhist story is about compassion for human life. It also has connections with 'The river goddess' (see Chapter 1) which likewise deals with the balance between our lives and the world around us.

This chapter links to Unit 3 of the SoW for Citizenship and could be covered in a single session or extended into a half-term project.

## Themes

Compassion, respect for other beings, choices

## Citizenship Scheme of Work

Unit 3 – Animals and us

## Aims

- To learn the meaning of compassion (or caring) and respect, for themselves, for other people and for animals.
- To understand that we all have an impact on the things around us and that helping others is the right choice to make.

## Resources

- The story on page 20
- The photocopiable sheets on pages 22 and 23

## About this religion

Siddhartha was a real man who left the comfort of his palace to journey the lands looking for truth. He found enlightenment and began to teach others about his findings. He was the first Buddha and he set down the original teachings which include these five promises:

1) Not to harm or kill living things, but to help others.
2) Not to steal or take things you have not been given, but to be generous.

3) Not to be greedy, but to be content.
4) Not to tell lies or speak unkindly, but to tell the truth.
5) To keep a clear mind – not drinking alcohol or taking drugs.

## Whole class starter

❑ Next ask the children the following questions, relating the discussion to any pets that they may have.

- What do animals need to stay healthy and happy? Suggest food and water, a comfortable place to sleep and love.

- What happens if animals don't get the things they need?

- Ask the children whether they think animals *need* love. Ask what might happen to an animal that is hurt or left alone for long periods.

❑ Explain that Buddhists believe all life is precious, from the smallest ant to humans. Say that the story they are about to hear is from the Buddhist religion.

❑ Read the story.

## Activities

❑ Ask the children the following questions:

- Why did Siddhartha want to stop Devadatta from taking the swan?

- What would have happened to the swan if she had gone to Devadatta?

- Did Siddhartha do the right thing, going to ask his father to settle the argument?

- Some of the king's advisers were on Siddhartha's side and some were on Devadatta's side. What do you think they were saying to him?

❑ Ask the children to decide which of the five promises Buddhists keep the story is about as you read. (It is primarily concerned with the first promise, although it also touches on the other promises.)

❑ Ask the children to draw a picture of a character from the story. Give out copies of page 22 and discuss the words on the sheet. Ask the children to label the character they have drawn with the appropriate words from the sheet, either cutting out the words and sticking them on or copying them.

❑ Ask the children to work in groups of three to re-enact the conversation between Siddhartha and Devadatta. The third child plays the swan, talking about how she thinks and feels during the argument.

❑ Show the children the pictures of people and animals on page 23. Tell them they are going to discuss the pictures in groups, and that at the end each group will present its ideas to the class. Give a copy of one picture to each group. Ask the groups to talk about what is happening in the picture and discuss whether it it is caring or non-caring. Ask what they would do in this situation. What would be the compassionate thing to do? Finally, bring the class back together and ask each group to present their ideas.

❑ Ask the children to write a thank you letter to someone who has shown them compassion. This could be a grandparent who sent them a present, a friend who visited when they were ill or their dog because they bring happiness! Encourage them to describe how they feel about the care that was shown to them.

## Differentiation

❑ More able children could do some research to make a collection of poems and stories about caring for animals. They could add pictures – their own or some downloaded from the internet.

❑ Less able children could fill out the gaps in a photocopy of a simple letter.

## Extension

❑ Ask the children if they know the story of the Ugly Duckling and, if so, ask some of them to retell it. Then ask them how they thought the Ugly Duckling felt. Did they think the ugly duckling was being bullied? Ask the children for words to describe some of the other animals in the story. These might include 'selfish', 'uncaring' and 'thoughtless'.

❑ Arrange for some live animals to be brought into the classroom. Get the children to draw pictures of them, focusing on just one part of the animal, like the nose, a feather or a paw. While they are drawing, ask the children what the differences are between animals and humans. Ask them to draw a comparison picture alongside the one they're drawing; for example, a human nose next to a beak, or a hand beside a paw. When the drawings are finished ask the children what similarities there are between animals and humans. You could suggest ideas such as: both feel pain, both eat and drink, both bleed, and so on.

## Plenary session

❑ At the end of the unit ask the children if they can remember the five promises of the Buddhist religion, and what the focus point of the story of Siddhartha and the Swan was.

❑ Ask the children if they think they would have done the same thing as Siddhartha when they first heard the story. If not, have they now changed their minds?

# Siddhartha and the swan

Have you ever heard the story of the Ugly Duckling? Well that's a bit like me, I wasn't much to look at when I was little but I've grown into a beautiful swan. My name is Srimoyie and I love nothing more than to fly high into the sky and swoop and glide with my brothers and sisters. I want to tell you about a very special man who saved my life. His name was Siddhartha.

Siddhartha was the son of a king and he was very clever – so clever that soon he knew more than his own teachers. He began to spend more and more time outdoors watching wildlife and learning about living things.

One day my family and I were flying across the lake and Siddhartha was sitting in his usual place enjoying the beautiful day. I remember I was looking down at him and thinking how peaceful he looked, when suddenly I felt a searing pain in my left wing. I clutched it to me and as I did I felt myself falling and falling, the air whistling past my face as the ground rushed towards me. I was so frightened. I tried to flap my wings again to stop my fall but I could no longer fly.

I hit the ground and found myself looking straight up into the eyes of Siddhartha.

"You poor thing," he whispered as he bent over and carefully lifted my limp body. "What has happened to you?" As he spoke he saw an arrow poking out from my wing – I had been shot down with a bow.

"Don't worry. I'll take care of you," Siddhartha continued. And with that he started towards his home, the palace.

Suddenly there was a cry from the bushes.

"Where are you going with that swan, Siddhartha? It's mine. I just shot it out of the sky. Give it to me!" It was Devadatta, Siddhartha's cousin. He had been out hunting, and wanted the swan to show his friends and family how clever he had been. "Come on now – hand it over!"

Can you imagine how scared I felt now? First I am rescued by a caring young boy, then another boy wants to take me away and kill me. I started to shake, and I believe Siddhartha felt my fear because he held me tighter and began to speak to Devadatta. I listened, frozen in his arms.

"I found this swan and it needs my help. I will not give it to you," said Siddhartha.

"But that is the swan that I shot from the sky. It's mine. I want it!"

"No, you will kill it," said Siddhartha.

"Give it to me!"

This time Devadatta really yelled at Siddhartha and they fell into a bitter argument. I was in so much pain. All I wanted was for them to let me sleep and be warm.

Once again Siddhartha seemed to read my mind because suddenly he began to walk towards the palace saying to his cousin, "This is getting us nowhere. We will go and ask my father." Devadatta agreed that this was the most sensible idea and all three of us – me in Siddhartha's arms – went into the palace to speak to the King.

The King ordered his ministers to come and listen to both sides of the argument. One said that because Devadatta had been the one who shot me out of the sky I should be given back to him. Then another said that as Siddhartha had been the one who found me he should keep me. I think the King became more confused than ever. He wanted to do the right thing but everyone had different ideas.

While they were all talking and arguing so sternly, a gentle voice spoke softly from the back of the room. Instantly everyone stopped and looked at a very old man standing in the doorway.

"Let me help you," he said. No one remembered seeing him there before, but I shall never forget his voice. It was calming and kind, and for the first time since I had been brought into the palace I felt safe. Even Siddhartha loosened his tight grip around my feathers.

The old man spoke again. "No living thing wants to feel pain or die. Do you not think that the swan bleeds and feels pain just as you or I do, Your Highness? Let the boy who would heal and care for the swan keep him. Do not give him to the boy who wants him dead."

Devadatta's eyes were on the King; he knew what the King's decision would be. Slowly, he turned and left the palace, without one glance at me and my limp wing. It was then that I realised I was finally safe. Siddhartha took me to a quiet room. He cleaned my wound and gave me food, water and a warm place to sleep while my wing healed.

One day Siddhartha entered the room and spoke to me in a gentle voice.

"I am going to take you back to the lake today. I have seen your family flying overhead and I believe your wing is strong now. You will be able to fly. Don't be afraid as I carry you out of this place."

He spoke so gently I had no need to fear him. We went down to the lake, back to the place where I had fallen. First I stretched out one wing. It felt good. Then I stretched the other. My feathers were brilliant white. I flapped my wings together and slipped silkily into the lake. My legs still felt strong and I remembered the first flight I had ever taken. When I heard my brothers and sisters overhead, I lifted up my neck and, beating my wings, I ran into the air, my legs pushing off the water. I was flying again, thanks to Siddhartha.

Siddhartha grew up to become a very great and compassionate man, and I would like to tell you more about him one day.

# The old man

| | | |
|---|---|---|
| uncaring | old | kind |
| selfish | caring | wise |
| clever | unkind | thoughtful |
| respected | scared | compassionate |

# Caring or not caring?

# CHAPTER 4

# The right choice – Christianity

This Christian story would work well coupled with the Islamic story of Ali's hajj (see Chapter 8), which also looks at moral choices and friendship. The lesson is designed to be spread over two or three lessons.

## Themes

Rights and wrongs, choices to keep us safe, moral choices

## Citizenship Scheme of Work

Unit 2 – Choices
Unit 4 – People who help us

## Aims

- To explore the concept of right and wrong when making decisions.
- To see how making the right choice in a situation can keep you safe from harm.

## Resources
- The story on page 26
- The photocopiable sheets on pages 28 and 29

## About this story from the Christian religion

This is a parable from the New Testament. Jesus tells the story to show that we are all defined by our actions. The Samaritans at the time were despised by most of the people who this story would have been aimed at, as apostates (those who formally renounced their religion), and so it would have had more impact on those it was told to. It would have an impact on racism - the Samaritan risked a lot to help the injured man.

## Whole class starter

❑ Ask the children if they have heard anyone use the phrase 'a good Samaritan'. If they have, do they understand what is meant by it? Ask if they have heard of the organisation the Samaritans and the service they provide. Explain a little about the work of the Samaritans telling the children that they are always there for anyone to ring up and talk about their problems. Tell the children that these modern day Samaritans are named after a kind man in a story in the Bible.

❑ Now read the story.

## Activities

❑ Ask the children the following questions:

- Why do you think the thieves were on this road?

- Was it a safe place for the traveller to be alone?

- What excuses did the first two men make for not helping the injured man?

- Do you think they were right not to help?

- Why do you think the Samaritan did stop and help?

❑ The story uses two words to describe the Samaritan's feelings when he saw the injured traveller: 'compassion' and 'sadness'. Ask the children if they understand what 'compassion' means. Ask if they think that it was this feeling that made the Samaritan stop and help.

❏ Next ask the children if they can think of some other situations where feeling 'compassion' would make them behave in a similar way:
  • if their friend was injured?
  • if their mum was struggling with the washing?

❏ Ask the children if there are any situations where they should not stop and help. Should the traveller have been on his own? The story tells us that the road was known for having thieves on it. Divide the class into small groups. Give each group a set of the photocopiable pictures on page 28 and ask them to sort them into three piles: 'Always help', 'Walk away' and 'Ask an adult for help'. When they have finished, bring the class back together to discuss their findings. Did all the groups organise the pictures in the same way? Did anyone decide to walk away from any of the situations?

❏ Ask the children why they think the traveller was attacked. Was it because he had a lot of money, or because of where he was travelling? Did he just look wrong? Do they think he would have been attacked if he had been with a group of people? Ask for suggestions for rules that could help to keep us safe, such as:
  • Don't go out alone after dark!
  • Keep away from strangers!
  • When you're out, stay with your friends!

❏ Once you have made a list of rules, give each child a copy of the poster template (page 29). Ask them to create a 'Keeping safe' poster, including a big heading, the list of rules and an eye catching picture.

## Differentiation

❏ More able children could create a poem to go with the posters, or write their own version of The Good Samaritan.

## Extension

❏ Discuss the types of issues phone help lines such as the Samaritans and Childline could help with. Would you ring up to talk about:
  • being bullied at school?
  • not being able to do homework?
  • feeling sad about losing a relative or pet?
  • not having fashionable clothes like your friends?

❏ Organise the children into pairs. One child pretends to be from a telephone help line, and the other calls up with a problem. Ask the child taking the call to be sympathetic and caring. Explain that the most important thing to do is to listen to what the other child has to say and try and find out what he or she really wants to do. The children should realise that it is more important to listen and be caring than to offer advice.

## Plenary session

❏ Ask the children to recall what they have learned from this section. Will they tell others about keeping safe? Make sure they understand they can take control of how safe they are by making the right choices. Explain that one of the reasons Jesus told this story was because of the way a lot of people at the time felt about the Samaritans, and that even though the injured man and the Samaritan were probably enemies, the Samaritan still did what was right.

### Note for the teacher

Prepare an assembly for the whole school based on this section. Include a dramatisation of the good Samaritan story. Use a narrator to tell the story while another child (or group of children) acts out the part of the traveller journeying on his own. The narrator stops the action and asks the audience what they think will happen next, and whether they think the traveller is safe. The narrator continues up to the point where the traveller is attacked. Finish the story with the two travellers who ignored the injured man and finally the Samaritan. Let the narrator explain that the Samaritan was a kind and compassionate man.

# The good Samaritan

NEWS JUST IN – THERE HAS BEEN YET ANOTHER ATTACK ON THE JERICHO ROAD – WIDELY BELIEVED TO BE THE WORK OF A GANG OF ROBBERS KNOWN LOCALLY AS THE 'JERICHO MOB'. WE GO LIVE TO OUR REPORTER AT THE SCENE...

"Good evening. I'm here with the innkeeper who first reported the incident. Now, sir, you say that an injured man was brought in here late last night by a Samaritan. Can you tell us what happened?"

"I can, I can! But first I'd just like to say that we sell lovely breakfasts here – all you can eat, and the missus makes a great cuppa..."

"I'm sure, but if you could just tell us what happened late last night...?"

"Oh yes, well, it was very late and we'd just put out all the oil lamps ready to go to bed, when there was a really loud banging on the front door. Well, as you can imagine, I thought it might be bandits, and the poor missus nearly fainted. So I grabbed the broom and slowly opened the door – but instead of bandits there were just two men standing there. Well, I say two men standing, it was actually one man standing – a Samaritan – and him virtually carrying the other, who, I might add, wasn't wearing anything but a cloak. Well, obviously I sent the missus straight upstairs. This man in the cloak was terribly battered and bruised, almost at death's door.

"I showed them right in, quickly banked up the fire and got them both something to eat. The Samaritan chap told me that he had found this poor man almost dying at the side of the road. I bet it was the Jericho Mob. Anyway the Samaritan thinks that he must have been there for hours. Everything he owned had been stolen, even his clothes! That's why the Samaritan had wrapped his own cloak around him and even taken the time and trouble to clean up his wounds, before finally bringing him here."

"And where is this Samaritan now? I'd like to talk to him? What's his name?"

"Well that's the funny thing. He was running really late for some important business, so he gave me some money for his friend – more than enough actually – and once I'd promised to take care of him, he rushed off!"

This is the story of the good Samaritan. It is well known. It is a story that Jesus told as an example for others to follow.

He told of the man travelling from Jerusalem to Jericho on a virtually deserted road. But there were villains watching the road and when there was no sign of anyone else around, the gang of bandits and thieves jumped out on the traveller. They stole everything and beat him so hard that they left him for dead.

A little later, another traveller came along the road. But instead of helping he crossed from one side of the road to the other to avoid the poor injured man. He told himself that this was none of his business.

Not long after that a second man appeared on the road but he told himself that it was wrong to get involved. He avoided the injured man, not even checking to see if he was alive or dead!

Finally a man from Samaria – a Samaritan – came by, travelling the same road. As soon as he saw the wounded man he went to him, with feelings of sadness and compassion. He tore strips from his clothing, covered him with his own cloak to keep him warm and took him to the nearest inn for help. Without the Samaritan's help the man would have died.

# What should I do?

# Poster template

### RULES TO HELP YOU STAY SAFE

...................................................................

...................................................................

...................................................................

...................................................................

...................................................................

# CHAPTER 5

# What's in the news? – Christianity

This chapter is based on the Christian story of 'The loaves and the fishes'. It has been written in the style of a newspaper report. It is designed to make children consider how stories are retold or reported in the media. It would work well alongside the Sikh story of 'Duni Chand and the needle of heaven' (see Chapter 15).

## Themes

Media influences, the importance of the news, alternative views, is there a right way to report an event?

## Citizenship Scheme of Work

Unit 11 – In the media – What's the news?

## Aims

• To look at how stories are reported in the media and how we are affected by them.
• To realise that there can be many different versions of events, depending on who tells the story, and that the media cover stories in different ways depending on their views.

## Resources

• The story on page 32
• The photocopiable sheets on pages 34 and 35
• Newspapers, magazines and comics
• Paper, pens, glue and scissors

## About this story

This Christian story is reported in all four gospels: Matthew 14: 13-22; Mark 6: 32-45; Luke 9: 10-17; John 6: 1-15. It might be worth asking the children to look up the different versions and compare them. The story emphasises the importance of the miracle. Jesus is said to have blessed the food publicly before sharing it out and then to have thanked God afterwards, again within sight of all the people.

## Whole class starter

❑ Explain to the children that the story 'The loaves and the fishes' is a Christian story. Ask them to pretend the story they are about to hear happened yesterday instead of 2,000 years ago. How many different ways would a story be reported today? (Newspaper, radio, television and the internet.) Ask them to imagine that they are listening to a news report of the story on the radio.

❑ Now read the story to the class.

## Activities

❑ Ask the children to think about what catches their eye when they are looking at newspapers and magazines. Share some out. Ask them to pick out the things that draw their attention. Discuss the layout of the papers and magazines. Ask which fonts are the most eye catching. Where does their eye naturally fall on the page? Which colours stand out?

❑ Next ask them to pick out headings from those that they think might lead to fun or exciting stories that they would want to read. What makes each story look appealing? Explain that if a story is presented in the right way people are more tempted to read it. Imaginative ideas can capture people's interest and draw them into an otherwise boring story.

❑ Look at the same story presented in two different newspapers. How is the story different? Are the pictures the same? Is the headline the same? (Try to compare a broadsheet with a tabloid.)

❑ Tell the children that they are going to design the front page of a newspaper reporting the loaves and fishes. Remind them of the papers they have just looked at. List some of the key points about a newspaper story on the board:
  • bold, eye catching format;
  • basic facts told using very few words;
  • exciting words;
  • eye catching pictures.

❑ Give each child a copy of the front page template (page 34) and ask them to design their own front page for the loaves and fishes story, displaying them on the wall once they are finished.

❑ Next, tell the children they are going to work in groups to present the story again, but this time as if it were a television news report. Some of them will be acting as characters from the story and others will be part of the news team, which could include a reporter, an assistant and camera person.

❑ Ask the children to organise a space where they can interview the characters. This can be as simple as a few chairs or you could set up a camera and television if you have the equipment. Suggest that they could choose to interview Jesus, one of his disciples or one of the people from the crowd. Remind them that each character will have their own viewpoint about what happened.

❑ Ask each group to make a list of questions for the reporter to ask. They should aim to come up with the best interview, by thinking up really interesting questions that everyone will want to know the answer to. Give them five minutes to practice before either videoing the interviews or simply performing them in front of the class.

## Differentiation

❑ More able children could look up and research the loaves and fishes story in the Bible, to see how the stories in each gospel differ.

❑ Less able children could see how many headlines they could come up with for other stories that they can find in the Bible.

## Extension

❑ To extend the activity, some members of the class could go on to produce a class newspaper, reporting stories from the Bible as if they had happened yesterday. Producing a whole paper gives the chance to look at the different people involved, from the editor to the printers. For those who are interested there is a wide choice of jobs, no matter what their talent or ability. You will need editors, reporters, photographers, layout designers and perhaps some illustrators.

❑ If possible, ask a journalist to come in and talk to the class. Ask the journalist to tell the class what sort of subjects they have reported, and how they decide what is really newsworthy.

❑ Give the children copies of Activity sheet 2 (page 35). They have to decide on six relevant scenes for a director to recreate for a television docu-drama. This activity could be done individually, in pairs or in groups.

## Plenary session

❑ Ask the children to think of one person who could have been by the lake shore. They could choose a member of the crowd (an old person or child or maybe a pickpocket), or they might prefer to be Jesus or one of his disciples. Ask them to retell the story of 'The loaves and fishes' from this person's point of view.

❑ Look at the different front pages produced in the lesson and comment on each before displaying them on the wall.

❑ After watching the interviews, discuss all of the different questions and techniques used for each interview. At the end take a vote on which was the most enjoyable.

# The loaves and the fishes

"TODAY ON THE SHORES OF THE SEA OF GALILEE A LARGE CROWD HAS COLLECTED TO HEAR THE TEACHINGS OF JESUS. JESUS AND A NUMBER OF HIS DISCIPLES, INCLUDING MARK, ARRIVED BY BOAT EARLY THIS MORNING. MANY HUNDREDS OF PEOPLE HAVE FLOCKED TO THE AREA, CROWDING ROUND FOR A BETTER VIEW OF JESUS, WHO HAS BEEN SPEAKING TO THEM FOR SEVERAL HOURS. OUR GALILEE REPORTER IS LIVE AT THE SCENE."

"Word of this man Jesus is spreading and, as you can see by the size of this crowd, people are willing to travel a long way to hear him. People have heard about the teachings of Jesus and also that he's worked miracles. Could it be that we are going to witness a miracle here today? The atmosphere is electric. People are hanging on this man's every word and the crowd

continues to grow. There must be thousands here, all eager to listen to the teachings of Jesus.

"It's getting late and the sun is low in the sky. I have been here for a couple of hours, but I am told that some of the people around me have been here since early morning, when Jesus arrived. Some parts of the crowd are growing restless and from where I am standing the disciples look a little on edge. One of them is whispering something to Jesus, perhaps suggesting that the people here will need to eat. I'm not sure about anyone else in the crowd but I know that I'm tired and getting hungry.

"Something is definitely happening down there. And in fact – yes – Jesus is asking the crowd if they need something to eat! But Mark doesn't look very happy; if anything I'd say he and the other disciples are looking more worried than before.

"I am picking my way down through the crowds now, closer to the action. Jesus has asked Mark to fetch some baskets from the boat. The baskets seem to contain food. I think – yes, I can see – just a moment – I can see 5 loaves of bread and 2 fish.

"Really, I can't believe what I am seeing but it seems that Jesus plans to feed the whole crowd from these

two baskets of food. Unbelievable! No wonder the disciples look a little worried!

"What's this? It seems that Jesus has told Mark to get everyone to sit down, and he and the other disciples are moving around the crowd asking everyone to sit – including me.

"This is just amazing. It appears that already half the crowd over on Jesus' left have got something to eat. Food is being passed around to everyone, and it's all come from nowhere.

"Thank you! I have just been given a large piece of bread and a tasty-looking piece of fish to go with it and, mmm... it's delicious! As I look around me everybody I see is eating. The people behind me are just getting theirs, and some of the people at the front actually appear to be having seconds. Again, I have to say this is unbelievable.

"Well, I came here hoping to witness a miracle and I have not been disappointed. Here, as I look around me, there is truly a miracle. Jesus wanted to feed five thousand people with just two small baskets of food but I am witness to the fact that everyone here has eaten, and eaten well. This man Jesus must be everything they say of him and more. I know that I for one will be keeping a close eye on him for the future."

# Newspaper template

Write in the headline and sketch the photo. Then cut out all the pieces and arrange them on a fresh sheet of paper to create your front page.

## THE Galilean Chronicle

*Since 1AD*

masthead

headline

photo

story

# Storyboard

You are going to create a docu-drama for television. Complete the storyboard below with pictures that tell the story of the loaves and fishes. Choose the most important parts of the story to show in each screen. The first screen has been done for you.

# Are we all the same? – Hinduism

> The story of 'Sumana sings' tells of a Hindu couple longing for a baby; something common to couples all over the world. The difference is the belief in their gods' ability to help them. The story helps children to recognise similarities and differences, and the activities offer a chance to explore these further. The story which would work well alongside either the Buddhist story of 'Thousand-armed Chenrezig' (Chapter 2) or the Jewish story 'The greatest gift of all' (Chapter 11).

## Themes

How are we all connected? Different places in the world, sameness, difference and diversity

## Citizenship Scheme of Work

Unit 1 – Taking part
Unit 5 – Diverse world

## Aims

To encourage children to think about:
• different places in the world and what they are like;
• how we are all connected in some way;
• diversity and how we are the same and different;
• to develop communication skills and self expression through discussion and participation.

## Resources

• The story on page 38
• The photocopiable sheets on pages 40 and 41

## About this religion

Hinduism is known as 'the Way' because it has a combination of beliefs, rites, customs and daily practices which the couple in the story would have followed in their simple lives. Accepting that life was an entrapment of misery and self-sacrifice (samsara), as the religion believes, is fundamental to the way the couple dealt with their longing for a baby. Lakshmi is the Hindu goddess of fortune, and Hindu people believe that if she visits them at Divali she will help them by granting their wishes. They believe that she will be found where there is goodness, truth and compassion.

Before reading it to the children, explain that the couple in the story really want to have a baby and have been waiting a long time for this to happen, but their faith has given them a positive attitude and they have never given up hope.

## Whole class starter

❑ Explain to the children that they are going to listen to a Hindu story which tells us about a Hindu goddess called Lakshmi. Tell them how she grants wishes at Divali when she finds goodness, truth and compassion.

❑ Ask the children what sort of people they think Lakshmi would help: someone who lives a good life and helps others, or someone who is lazy and selfish?

❑ Ask the children what wish they would want the goddess to grant. How would they convince her that they deserved her help?

❑ Now read the story.

## Activities

❑ Ask the children the following questions:

1. Why did Deepak think Lakshmi did not visit them?

2. Was their house run down because they were lazy and did not care, or for some other reason?

3. Did being poor give Deepak and Sumana fewer rights than other Hindus?

4. What was Deepak and Sumana's wish? How do you think they felt about not having a baby? Do you think being a Hindu made them feel any differently from other couples in the same situation?

❑ The words 'grace', 'charm' and 'loveliness' are often used when talking about Lakshmi. Ask the children to draw a picture of Lakshmi, trying to show these qualities without actually using the words. Let them work in pairs to do this. Ask them to look at each other's faces and pull an ugly angry face and then a happy lovely face. Ask them to use the happy expression as a model for Lakshmi's face. Ask the children to move around the room in a clumsy way, then a graceful way, and think about how they can show this in the picture. Finally ask them to think of charming things to say to each other, and ask them to add a speech bubble to their finished picture to show charm.

❑ In groups, the children could design, colour and build a lamp for Divali. The lamp needs to include symbols to represent the goddess Lakshmi and should be brightly coloured to attract attention. Each group needs to discuss, agree and build either one group lamp or similar individual lamps.

❑ Ask the children what song they would sing for the goddess Lakshmi, asking her to visit and grant her wish. Explain that singing is a way of communicating that is very good for expressing feelings without needing many words. Demonstrate this by playing three different types of music, either from a CD or on different instruments.

❑ The children could conduct an enquiry into how other communities function, and could compare their own to one in India, using the internet and videos to help with the research.

❑ Give the children copies of Activity sheet 1 (page 40) and ask them to compare two people, to find out how they are the same and how they are different. You could ask them to continue on the back of the sheet, detailing the similarities and differences in their hobbies, home life and festivals.

## Differentiation

❑ More able children could write a poem to go with their picture of Lakshmi.

## Extension

❑ The children who made lamps could go into another class and show them to the children there, then help them to build some of their own.

## Plenary session

❑ Ask the children what Deepak and Sumana had in common with couples in this country, and then ask them what was different about them. Discuss how the story could have been told about a couple in this country: would it have been more clinical and had hospitals in it? Do you think there would have been as much hope from a Western couple? Finally ask the children to complete the questionnaire on page 41.

# Sumana sings

"I want this to be the best Divali ever!" said Deepak to his wife as he hung up another lantern. Sumana did not hear him. She was too busy singing to herself, just as she always did. All the while she cleaned their meagre cottage, hoping that the goddess Lakshmi would choose to visit their home this year. The couple longed for a baby and they longed for the goddess to enter their home and grant their wish.

Sumana and Deepak struggled through each year with only just enough to eat. The soil around their home was poor and the crops they grew hardly fetched any money at market. But still, they had each other and this made them happy. If Deepak was feeling sad, Sumana only needed to sing to him to bring a smile back to his face. In fact, when Sumana sang, everyone stopped to listen. She had a magic in her voice that even the birds could hear.

Secretly Deepak wondered if the reason Lakshmi never visited their home was because it was so small and crumpled, with a hole in the roof, and because they could not afford the brightly coloured lamps that other homes displayed. Lakshmi, the goddess of fortune and wealth, was known to be the height of loveliness, grace and charm. So Deepak could understand why she would not want to enter such a tattered house.

As he pondered on what he could do to make their little house attractive to the great Lakshmi, wife of Vishnu, he found himself once again entranced by his wife's singing. It was then that he had an idea.

While Sumana cleaned inside, he busied himself building a platform just outside the door. What with all the banging, Sumana came outside to see what was going on. Deepak explained that he wanted Sumana to sit outside and sing, and keep singing into the night.

As she climbed up onto the platform, a little confused, Deepak lit the lanterns. Then Sumana began to sing. She sang every song that she could remember, even those she had learned as a child, and Deepak waited by her side throughout the long night. Late in the night he thought he heard an owl. Could it be Ulooka, Lakshmi's owl? Was Lakshmi on her way?

Ulooka flew swiftly through the night and called Lakshmi to come and listen.

When the goddess heard the purity of Sumana's voice she made her way into the cottage at once.

"Such a beautiful song," she thought, as she made her way into Deepak and Sumana's little home, "I will visit here again."

The following year Sumana gave birth to a son – Lakshmi had granted the couple their wish. She brought them more good fortune, too. Deepak found the soil much easier to work and it was much richer. The vegetables were now the first to sell at market, which meant that he could afford to mend the roof of their house.

At the next Divali Deepak and Sumana were able to decorate with many brightly coloured lanterns. But even with the lanterns, Sumana knew the only real way to say 'thank you' for their good fortune was to sing through the night, with Deepak by her side.

Name _____

# Same/different

Choose two people you know well and complete the chart below to show
how they are the same but different. One of the people could be you.
Draw their pictures in the boxes and write their names underneath.

| | | |
|---|---|---|
| | _____ | _____ |
| Feelings | | |
| Food | | |
| Clothes | | |
| Music | | |
| Sense of humour | | |
| Religion | | |

PHOTOCOPIABLE

Name  _____

# Sumana sings – quiz

1. List three things that you have in common with everyone else.

   ..........................   ..........................   ..........................

2. List three things about you that are different from Sumana and Deepak.

   ..........................   ..........................   ..........................

3. What was Deepak and Sumana's religion?

   ......................................................................................

4. What is Lakshmi the goddess of?

   ......................................................................................

5. What did Deepak and Sumana wish for?

   ......................................................................................

6. Write down the names of two other religions.

   ..............................................   ..............................................

7. Draw a picture of Ulooka, Lakshmi's owl.

# CHAPTER 7

# Democracy in school – Hinduism

> This chapter is based on the Hindu story 'Prince Prahlad and the demon king'. The main group of activities work well as one ongoing project focusing on Unit 10 and would be suitable for a complete half term's work.

## Themes

Democracy, trust and belief in God to conquer evil, rules and law

## Citizenship Scheme of Work

Unit 5 – Living in a diverse world
Unit 8 – How do rules and laws affect me?
Unit 10 – Local democracy for young citizens

## Aims

- To learn about Hindu and Indian culture and be aware of differences from our own.
- To learn about democracy and how it should benefit us all.
- To learn how to run a democratic campaign.

## Resources

- The story on page 44
- The photocopiable sheets on pages 46 and 47

## About this religion

Hindu's believe in many Gods. Prahlad was one of them. The reality between fact and imagination is blurred with real–life historic characters and events which became muddled with myth and reality. Hindus believe that the way to obtain freedom is to be emptied of every sense of self-realisation (Brahman).

## Whole class starter

❑ Explain in simple terms the difference between democracy and dictatorship. The first is where the people vote for their leaders, the second is where they do not; their leader is presented to them, often an officer from the army or someone supported by the army. Ask the children which system they think they would prefer to live under. Ask if they think one way is better or fairer than the other.

❑ Explain that the story you are going to read is a Hindu story about a king who became an evil demon and ordered everyone around him to do what ever he said.

❑ Now read the story.

## Activities

❑ Ask the children the following questions:

- What wish did the gods grant the king? Why?

- Do you think that he abused this wish? Do you think he was always a bad man? If not, what made him change?

- Was the village a democracy or a dictatorship?

- Did the villagers obey the demon because they liked and respected him? If not, why did they obey him?

- What would have happened if the demon king had never been killed? Could the King's rule have affected the rest of the world? Ask the children if they can think of a leader in recent times who became a dictator. Explain in simple terms about Hitler and World War 2.

❏ Tell the children that there is going to be a class election. Explain that it involves a lot of work, campaigns and policies. It will end with a secret ballot when one person will be elected to stand for the class.

❏ Week 1: Split the class into four or five groups. Ask which child from each group would like to put themselves forward for election. The group needs to choose someone who has good ideas, who is good at communicating and who can listen to others. If necessary, choose one child for them. Explain that each group will campaign to help its candidate win. Ask each group to decide on policies and a name for their group. Explain what is meant by policies; ask the children what sort of things they think the class needs. What could their candidate try to change if they were elected – ask for a tuck shop, more play equipment or a buddy scheme? Ask each group to use the Activity sheet on page 46 to write down what their policies are and design a logo for their group.

❏ Week 2: Ask the groups to make posters and badges to publicise their candidate and policies. Discuss why this is important.

❏ Week 3: Ask a local MP or council member to come and talk to the class and explain a little about how a campaign would be run. Discuss how each group would put their policies into practice. Are they ideas that can actually work? Ask the groups to question each other to find out who has ideas that can be put into action.

❏ Week 4: Set up a debate between the groups, giving all a chance to question each other's policies. Show the class a video of Prime Minister's Questions to give them a taste of how to question each other. Ask each group to write a short speech for their candidate to give, convincing everyone to vote for them.

❏ Week 5: Ask the candidates to deliver their speeches to the whole class, one at a time. Now hold the ballot. Before children cast their votes, explain that adults vote to choose governments and local councils. Explain that one day it will be their right to vote to say what kind of government they want. Make it clear that this is a secret ballot, and that everybody is free to vote as they choose. Give every child a copy of a ballot paper (from page 47). Ask them to mark their votes and bring them to you, or get some older children to come in to run the vote and act as impartial observers.

## Differentiation

❏ Higher achievers could research different policies by looking up the manifestos of the different political parties on the internet.

❏ Lower achievers could be the ones encouraged to check the spellings on the policy sheets by using dictionaries.

## Plenary session

❏ Use the announcement of the vote to conclude this section of work. Ask the elected candidate to give a speech and explain what they are going to do next. Ask if they are going to be fair, as in a democracy, or turn into the demon king. What will the other children do if their representative stops listening to the class and only does what he or she wants?

❏ Ask the children what they thought happened in Prahlad's village once the demon was defeated. Would someone have needed to take charge?

❏ Find out if the class enjoyed the election campaign. Are they looking forward to voting when they get older?

# Prahlad and the demon king

"Do as I tell you! I am King. I am protected by the gods and cannot be killed. You will do what I say or DIE!"

It was true, or so it seemed, that the demon king could not be killed. Many had tried and been tortured for it.

A long time ago the king had been a man called Hiranya Kaship, who was devoted to the gods. He had prayed day and night, and because of this devotion the gods had granted him a wish.

"I wish that I will never die!" he said. So they granted him this:

> "You will not die in the day or night,
>
> Nor inside nor out.
>
> You will not die by the hand of man,
>
> Nor of god nor animal.
>
> You will not be killed by any weapon,
>
> Nor on the ground nor in the air."

"I must be a god," Hiranya Kaship thought to himself, knowing that he could never die. So he stopped worshipping and praying and became more evil with every passing year, treating his people like slaves or worse.

So there you are, you see – impossible to kill him. The people of my village had no choice but to obey his selfish orders. He was evil and so was his sister Holika. As children we hid whenever they walked the streets. It was a miserable life and we lived in fear, playing only at dusk and dawn when

nobody was about. There was not enough food to eat and the demon king (as we called him in secret) did nothing to help us. He said it was our fault that the gods did not care for us the way they had cared for him.

One morning I spoke to my mother as she was placing her bindi on her forehead.

"I am so hungry, mother. Can't we go to the king and ask for some food?" My mother looked at me with her sad dark eyes reflecting her dull and faded sari.

"We are powerless, my son. All we can do is pray that one day Vishnu will help us."

I believe that Prince Prahlad must have heard our prayers. He was Hiranya Kaship's son and he grew up to hate his father and his evil ways. Prahlad was a good man who followed the Hindu faith. He prayed every day to the god Vishnu and would help us in any way he could.

One hot sticky morning a blood-curdling cry came from the palace windows – "I will have his head! No longer will he torment me. No longer will he disobey me. He will die!" As we looked up to the palace we saw Prahlad, the king's own son being dragged from the doors towards a deep pit. We could not believe our eyes. The king had ordered his own son to be put to death.

As we watched, Prahlad stayed calm. There was a low and constant hissing coming from the pit. It was full of the most poisonous snakes you have ever seen. There was no hope for Prahlad. But as the tears burst from my eyes, Prahlad himself stayed calm. As he was thrown into the pit he prayed aloud to Vishnu. The demon king watched gleefully, waiting for the fatal painful bite that would be the end of his son. We watched. We waited. There was no sound, no scream of agony, not even the sound of hissing. As Prahlad had fallen to the bottom of the pit, the snakes had simply fallen asleep. Vishnu had answered Prahlad's prayer.

We were all very relieved, but not the Demon King. He was furious.
Next, Prahlad was taken to an open field and tied to the ground. A herd of elephants was beaten and chased towards Prahlad. Once again he prayed to Vishnu. The demon king waited, eager to see his son trampled to death, but as the elephants moved across the field they simply stepped over Prahlad, each one of them missing him completely. Again Prahlad was left unharmed.

The Demon King screamed, "This cannot be. This will not be. I shall see you die a most horrible, horrendous and painful death. Your god will not save you this time." He ordered a huge bonfire to be built and told his sister Holika to help him. She too had magical powers, which kept her safe from fire and flames. Holika grabbed Prahlad and bundled him into the flames. We believed that this time, inside the fire, he was surely dying. Vishnu had other ideas and kept Prahlad safe once more. Instead of Prahlad screaming from the flames, it was Holika's voice we heard as the flames took her – her magic was not as strong as Vishnu's powers.

"Where is this God that protects you? I will kill him and then no one can stop me from killing you. Where is he? Where is he?"

The demon king's face had turned red, but still Prahlad remained calm.

"He is everywhere," answered Prahlad.

"Is he in that bush?" the demon king laughed. "Is he in that rock?"

"Yes!" answered Prahlad once again. "Vishnu is everywhere."

"So he is in that pillar then?" And with this, he rushed towards the pillar and raised his massive sword bringing it down on the pillar with an angry blow. At this moment Vishnu appeared, with the claws and head of a lion and the body of a man. The king turned and ran through the glowing red dusk to the palace. Before he could put more than one foot through the door, the mighty creature picked up the Demon King and tore him apart with his lion's claws. The demon was dead.

Vishnu had saved our village from the terrible torrent of evil. Prahlad's faith had been so great that it had brought about the triumph of good over evil. And once again my friends and I were able to eat until our bellies were full!

# Our group

## Our policies

- 

- 

- 

- 

- 

Our logo

# Ballot papers

**CANDIDATE** tick one only

⬜ ⬜ ⬜ ⬜ ⬜

**CANDIDATE** tick one only

⬜ ⬜ ⬜ ⬜ ⬜

**CANDIDATE** tick one only

⬜ ⬜ ⬜ ⬜ ⬜

**CANDIDATE** tick one only

⬜ ⬜ ⬜ ⬜ ⬜

# A true friend – Islam

This chapter looks at the Muslim story, 'Ali's hajj'. It encourages children to think about making the right choices. The activities can spread over one or more sessions. This story makes a good pair with the Christian story of the good Samaritan (see Chapter 4).

## Themes

Self sacrifice, friendship, life as a journey

## Citizenship Scheme of Work

Unit 2 – Choices
Unit 12 – Moving on

## Aims

- To help children understand the meaning of friendship and sacrifice.
- To help children understand the idea of making moral choices.
- To help children begin to see life as a journey where changes are constant and to observe their progression along it, as through the school years.

## Resources

- The story on page 50
- The photocopiable sheets on pages 52 and 53
- String or ribbon of different colours and/or different coloured beads

## About this religion

Muslims believe in one God and live their lives according to the Qur'an which was written down by the prophet Mohammad. Mohammad's fundamental vision was that all people should become one single community (umma), all looking out for one another.

## Whole class starter

❑ Tell the children the title of the story and explain to them that the word *hajj* is an Arabic word that means 'pilgrimage'. Ask them if they know what a pilgrimage is. Take time telling them about pilgrimages and how people of many different religions go on them. Explain that some people make pilgrimages to fulfil religious vows and some because they believe that the sick can be cured by visiting a holy place. Ask if they can think of a special place that some people go to. You could suggest Rome, Lourdes or Varanasi.

❑ Explain that the character in the story can only make his pilgrimage (his *hajj*), by saving for a long time. Ask the children to think of something that they really want that would cost a lot of money. Then ask if they think they would still want that thing in six months or in two years. What about in 20 years time – would it still be worth saving for all that time? Thinking this far ahead is quite a difficult concept for many children at this age. The thing that they want now is the most important.

❑ Now read the story.

## Activities

❑ Ask the children the following questions:

- What was Ali's dream? What was his sacrifice?

- Why was it such a big sacrifice for Ali to give his money to Hassim?

- How had Ali lived his life up to this point?

- Did he believe he was disobeying his religious beliefs?

- Had it been easy for him to save the money for his *hajj*?

- Think of a time when you have made a sacrifice for someone. What would you do for your best friend?

❑ Divide the children into small groups and give each group a copy of page 52. Explain that they are going to make a game about life's journey. In the game you have to get from point A (the beginning) to point B (the end), but along the way there will be some difficulties to overcome.

❑ Ask the children to think back to the story to see if they can remember some of Ali's problems. Remind them that saving his money meant that sometimes he had to miss out on things, like the camel racing. Sometimes he could not save at all because of important repairs to his house. All these things were problems he had to overcome.

❑ The children must first decide on the journey for the game and its title. If any find this really difficult they could just follow the story of Ali's *hajj*, but encourage them to think of a different situation. You could also suggest the journey from reception into juniors, or learning to swim.

❑ Finally they must decide on the wording for the squares. Some squares will have a negative outcome, like "You forgot your homework! Go back three spaces," or "Too scared to get in the water! Miss a turn." Others will have a positive outcome: "Today you made three new friends. Move to space 9," or "You swam without armbands. Have another throw!"

❑ While making the games, talk to the children about any worries or concerns they might have had in their lives. Do they get worried about moving to a new class each year? Do changes and new situations worry them or excite them?

❑ Finally test the games by playing them with dice. If there is time, move the games around the groups to see which are successful and can be understood.

## Extension

❑ Divide the class into small groups. Tell them they are going to make some friendship bracelets. Give each group a copy of page 53, which explains how each colour in the bracelet represents a different quality, and asks them to design a bracelet and then colour it. Talk about the qualities they look for in friends. Let them decide who they are going to make their bracelet for. Make sure they understand that the colour and design of the bracelet they make should correspond to the person they are making it for. (Boys may prefer to use knotted coloured string rather than beads, but the concept is the same.)

## Differentiation

❑ Ask more able children to write about saving for that really important item that was talked about in the beginning of the lesson. Ask them to consider what they would go without to get it, and what it would mean to them to have saved on their own and accomplished their task.

❑ Less able children could attempt the same idea but with a writing frame to help them.

The thing that I would like to save for is…

I want this because…

If I achieved my goal I would feel…

## Plenary session

❑ Ask the children why they think Ali came to the decision that he did. In the end what was really important to him? Can they think of a time when they had the chance to help someone? Is it important to sacrifice things for other people? What are the most important things in life? How do we judge when someone really needs help?

# Ali's hajj

My name is Ali. I am a very old man now, not long for this world, so it is important for me to tell you my story. I am a Muslim and I have lived a humble and obedient life, following the laws set down by Muhammad.

From an early age I set my sights on making pilgrimage or hajj, as it is called, to Makkah. This is what the prophet Muhammad commanded every Muslim to do – if they could afford it – and it became my dream. Of course I would afford it. I would make sure I could. I would save and save all my life if I had to.

So I vowed that every month I would put away a little of what I earned. I can't say that it was easy. Some months my friends would ask me to go with them and race camels, other times I would need money to buy a gift. I am sure you can all think of something that you would like to spend your money on – sweets or a toy or game – but I always made sure that I put something away.

It took me many, many years to save. There were some real disasters. Sometimes there was not enough food. Another time I had to rebuild my home. But I knew that one day I would have enough to make my journey. And that thought, my dream, helped me to stay positive throughout my life.

At last I had saved enough. My skin was wrinkled and my hands callused from years of labour. But my mind – well it was full of excitement. After years of waiting and believing, my time had come.

I laid out special new clothes, ready to wear, and sat contemplating the journey. The journey I was about to make and the journey my life had taken to get me to this point.

The night before I left I went to say goodbye to my good friend and neighbour, Hassim. But when I knocked there was no reply. I couldn't leave without seeing him, so I decided to go in.

"Hello, it's Ali!" I called. But still no reply. I thought I would leave Hassim a note, so I looked around for some paper. As I was looking I heard a moan from the back room. There, lying on the bed, was my friend. He looked so sick.

"Why have you no medicine?" I cried. "Why has the doctor left you no medicine?"

My friend told me that the doctor had not come, and would not be coming, because he had no money to pay him. This news shocked and worried me. I made Hassim as comfortable as I could, but as I left him sleeping it was clear to me that without help from a doctor my friend would die.

I returned home to make the last preparations for my hajj. As I put my things into my bag I looked in my purse and realised that there was more than enough money to pay for a doctor and medicine for Hassim – but if I give Hassim the money for the doctor I would not have enough left to make the hajj. I stared at my savings long into the night. I would never be able to save that amount of money again. This really was my last chance to go to Makkah, but the money could save Hassim's life. Should I sacrifice my life's dream or follow Muhammad's command? What would you do?

### (STOP READING AND THINK WHAT YOU WOULD DO)

At first light I opened my door and set off. It didn't take me long to reach the doctor and on the way I saw many people starting off on their hajj. Hassim recovered quickly once he had the medicine.

Did you make the same decision as me?

When my neighbours returned from Makkah they ran up to me, shouting "How did you get home before us?"

As you can imagine I was a little confused and tried to explain that I had never actually left.

"Nonsense!" they replied. "We saw you circle the Ka'bah. We saw you in your white robes on the plain of Arafat!"

You see, Allah had seen my sacrifice, and because I gave my money to Hassim, he saw to it that I went on hajj anyway – in spirit. I have been at peace ever since. I did the right thing and it turned out for the very best.

# Journey game

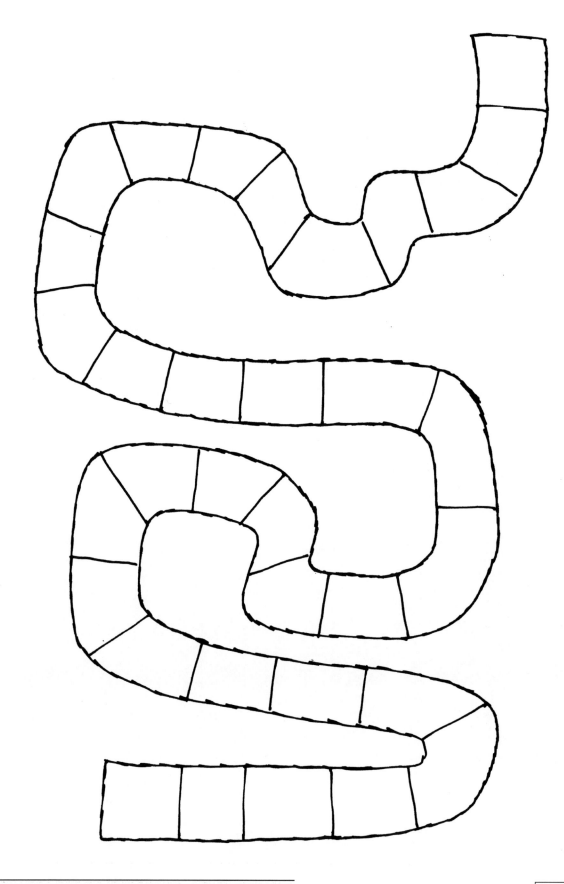

Name _____

# Friendship bracelets

**red** = loving

**yellow** = funny

**blue** = caring

**green** = loyal

**pink** = understanding

**black** = good listener

**white** = honest

**orange** = giving

**purple** = thoughtful

Use the information about friendship bracelets above to design and colour a bracelet for someone you know.

# CHAPTER 9

# Who needs rules? – Islam

This chapter is based on the Muslim story 'King Hakim's Garden' about a king who seems to have very little regard for the needs of others. It explores ideas about people's rights and respect for others. It could be used alongside the Hindu story 'Prince Prahlad and the demon king' (see Chapter 7).

## Themes

The law and authority, actions and consequences, individual needs

## Citizenship Scheme of Work

Unit 8 – How do rules and laws affect me?
Unit 9 – Respect for property

## Aims

- To recognise the consequences of stealing from others and how it affects the victim and offender.
- To recognise that individuals have different needs and that these needs must be respected.
- To understand why rules and laws are needed, and that someone is needed to oversee them.

## Resources

- The story on page 56
- The photocopiable sheets on pages 58 and 59

## About this religion

The noun 'Islam' means peace and stands for entering into a condition of tranquillity and security with God through allegiance and surrender to him. Muslims must live their lives according to the law of God and will only enter his kingdom if they have followed his laws. The story of King Hakim is one that might be told around the time of Ramadan when Muslims must prepare by remembering their sins and asking for forgiveness.

## Whole class starter

❑ Ask the class if they can list some school rules. How do they know about these rules? Are they written on posters somewhere? Or have they just been told them? Are they just common sense? Then ask the children if they understand and agree with the rules. Can they explain the rules? Explain that many are for the benefit of the whole school – for example, 'No running' is sensible because you could bump into someone, knock books or a drink out of someone's hand or fall over! If any children don't agree with the rules, ask them to explain why.

❑ Ask the children if they think they would behave correctly without rules being in place. Do they think everyone would be respectful of each other? Brainstorm what the word 'respect' means and then give the children copies of Activity sheet 1 (page 58). Ask them to circle each of the words that is 'respectful' and colour it green like leaves on the tree. They should colour the other words brown, then use each of the respectful words in a sentence to make the trunk and branches of the tree.

❑ Next explain to the class that you are going to read them a story about a king who always took what he wanted without thinking of the rights and wrongs of his actions. Before you read the story ask if any of the children can think of a time when they have done something similar to this?

❑ Now read the story.

## Activities

❑ Ask the children the following questions.

• What did the king do that was wrong?

• Did the king believe that he had to follow rules?

• Are rules meant for everyone to follow, or just for some?

• What happens if people choose to ignore what is right and just do what they want?

• Why did the woman not just take the gold? What do you think you would have done?

• If an older child needed a pen, saw yours and just took it, how would you feel? What if they offered to pay you 20p? Would that make a difference? What if it was a special pen and you could not replace it?

❑ Organise the children into groups of three. Give each group a copy of one of the situation cards on page 59. Ask two of the children to role play the people shown on the card and the third to act as mediator, like the Qadi in the story, to sort out the problem. This could also be done in larger groups, asking more than one person to act as mediator, or by putting one of the groups in front of the class and asking everyone for suggestions to settle the dispute.

❑ Ask the children if they think the king was actually stealing from the woman. Did he think that he was stealing? Ask them what stealing is. Did the king need the widow's garden? Did he take her feelings and needs into consideration? Explain that you want them to write a letter from the widow in the story to her best friend. The letter should explain how she felt when the king came to her garden and decided to take it.

❑ Ask the children to write down why the king was wrong to take the widow's garden. Give them the first line, "What the king did was wrong because…" Also ask them to include these points: how the widow felt; was it a kind or a selfish thing to do?; how the king felt at the end of the story.

## Extension

❑ Set up a courtroom role play. Choose one of the situation cards or think of a new situation. Choose children to play the parts of the judge, jury and lawyers. Ask a group to act out the situation from the card and then put each of the characters in the 'dock', to answer questions from the lawyers. Give each lawyer five minutes with the different witnesses to work out appropriate questions to ask – this will need quite a lot of adult input! Finally ask the jury for their opinions on who they think is in the right.

## Differentiation

❑ More able children could also write a letter from the king to the woman to try and say sorry and make up for his behaviour. Alternatively, they could write down a list of punishments for the king to try to compensate the widow for his actions.

❑ Less able children could act out the conversation between the widow and her friend, or the conversation between the widow and the king instead of writing a letter.

## Plenary session

❑ Ask the children how they would feel if they saw someone take something that was not theirs. Ask them to compare stealing a sweet with stealing a bicycle. Is one worse than the other? Explain that there are always different degrees of things and it is important to discover why someone has done the wrong thing. Maybe someone stole food because they were hungry and had no money. The act of stealing is still wrong but the punishment may be different.

❑ Who is affected by stealing? Ask the children what actions they could take if they saw another person stealing. Ask them to think about different situations. What would they do if it was an adult? a toddler? a friend?

# King Hakim's garden

King Hakim had one of the most beautiful gardens in the land. It was peaceful, with lawns cut short and sweet smelling flowers. At one side there was a pond with an elegant fountain, and on the other a pergola. Underneath there was a shady seat where the king would sit and watch the day.

The king's garden overlooked a smaller garden. This garden was not so pleasing to the eye. It was scruffy and overgrown with hardly any flowers. One day the king decided that he did not want to look at the untidy garden any longer.

"Send my courtiers to find out who owns that garden, and give them enough gold to buy it at once," said the king. So the courtiers went, but the answer they brought back to the king was not what he was expecting.

"What do you mean, they would not sell? I'm the king. Take more gold, they will have to sell."

But once again the courtiers returned with the same message. There was no sale. By this time the king was becoming angry.

"I'll go myself," he insisted. And so he set off to meet the owner of the garden.

The owner of the small, overgrown piece of land was a widow who had lived there most of her life. At first she had lived there with her husband when they were newly wed. After her husband had died she had lived there all alone.

"Please, your Majesty," she begged, "this garden is my life. I have always grown my vegetables here to sell at market. I am too old to change now. This is where my heart lies, in the ground I tend everyday."

But the king was not listening. If he wanted something he would have it.

"If the woman will not leave, then you will just take down the fence and dig up those ugly vegetables anyway. I have offered more in gold than is fair."

With this the king ordered his soldiers to work. The woman was frantic. She rushed away to find a qadi – a judge – who might be able to help her save her garden.

When the qadi arrived the king spoke to him respectfully, even asking his advice on what to build on his new piece of land. The qadi needed time to think. He could see how selfish and unfair the king was being but how could he say this to King Hakim? Finally he asked the king if he could speak to him and offer advice about the land the following morning. The king agreed, feeling very proud that the qadi was taking such an interest in his garden, and told everyone to stop work until the following morning. The woman was relieved and she hoped that the qadi would find a way to help her keep her beloved garden.

PHOTOCOPIABLE

The next morning everyone assembled once more and awaited the arrival of the qadi. It was not long before he was spotted, but he was not alone. This time he arrived with a donkey.

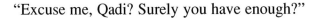

"I wanted to ask your majesty if I could take some sacks of soil from your garden?" said the qadi.

"Why, of course, Qadi!" answered the King, a little surprised by the qadi's request. "Please take what you want. My soldiers will help you."

So the qadi loaded a sack of soil onto his wobbly donkey. Then he added another, and then another until the poor donkey felt his knees knocking. Still the sacks of soil kept being loaded onto the donkey, until finally, much to the donkey's relief, the king spoke up.

"Excuse me, Qadi? Surely you have enough?"

"But I want more!" replied the qadi, heading to the poor donkey with yet another sack. By this time the donkey was just about ready to sit down.

"Qadi, I know you to be a wise man. So why take more soil than you can possibly carry away?" asked the king. Everybody looked at the qadi and the old widow waited eagerly for the qadi to reply.

"Your majesty, isn't that just what you have done by taking this woman's garden?"

Looking a little confused the king replied that he did not understand.

"What do you need with this garden, your Majesty? You already have a garden that is far too big to walk around in a single day! When we die, your majesty, do we not face Allah with all of our sins?" The king nodded. "Then think of the soil as representing our sins! Do you expect Allah to forgive you on Judgement Day if you arrive with more sins than you can carry? Will he allow you to pass into paradise?"

The whole garden fell silent. Then King Hakim, realising his error, fell to his knees.

"May Allah forgive me! I have been so selfish. To think that I was prepared to take what I wanted without a thought for anyone else. I will not take the garden. But how can I repent for my sin? Help me, Qadi!"

"You must ask the woman for forgiveness and put right this terrible mess – and unload my poor donkey!" replied the qadi.

So the king set about compensating the woman for what he had done. He unloaded the donkey and told the soldiers to replant all the vegetables. He felt so ashamed that he sent the woman a full chest of gold. She willingly forgave the king as he had learned his lesson, but she also asked him to build a brand new stable for the qadi's donkey.

Name _____

# The respect tree

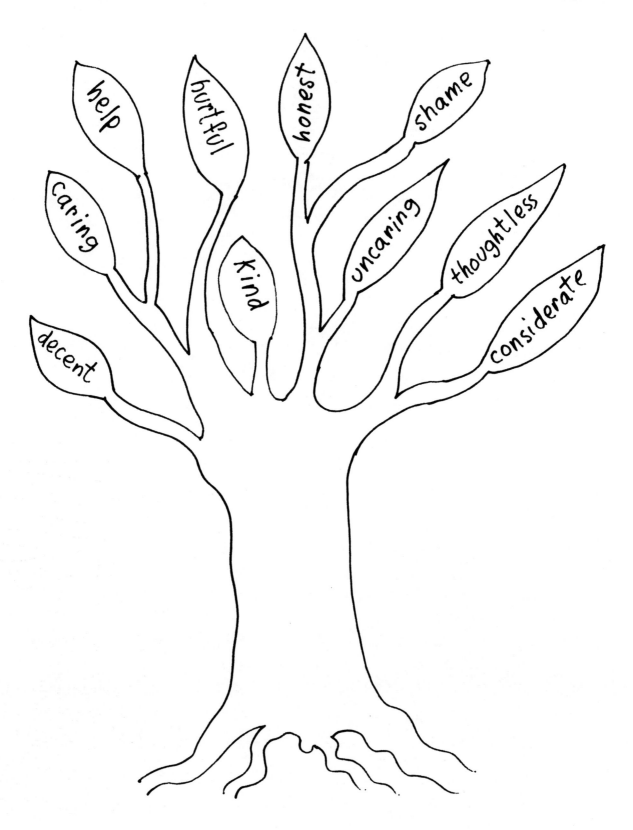

# Situation cards

# CHAPTER 10

# Your rights – Jainism

This chapter is based on a Jainist story called 'Mairavati'. Mairavati believed that her life was completely controlled by karma and so surrendered herself to it, and in doing so was able to stand up for what she believed to be the truth. The story would work well alongside the Jewish story of 'Moses in the bullrushes' (see Chapter 12). It links to Unit 7 of the Citizenship SoW.

## Themes

Human rights, standing up for what we believe in, karma and self belief

## Citizenship Scheme of Work

Unit 7 – Children's rights; human rights

## Aims

- To discover that we must be true to ourselves and that we all have rights.
- To learn that we should be prepared to stand up for our rights and what we believe in.

## Resources

- The story on page 62
- The photocopiable sheets on pages 64 and 65

## About this religion

The Jain religion was founded in the 6th century BC in India in protest against Hinduism. Jain believe in karma (the cause and effect of desire) which means that the lives we live now are directly affected by how we lived and behaved in past lives. Jains must refrain from violence and follow these rules known as the Three Jewels:

1 – right faith;
2 – right cognition;
3 – right conduct.

## Whole class starter

❑ Explain to the children that they are going to listen to a story from the Jain religion. The story is about a princess who has very strong beliefs. Her father expects her to ignore those beliefs for him. Ask the children what they think the princess will do. Will she simply obey her father or stay true to herself? Remind the children that her father is a king. Ask them if they think it is important to always do what other people say. Say that the word 'karma' is used in the story and explain what it means.

❑ Now read the story.

## Activities

❑ Ask the children the following questions.

- Why did the king get angry with Mairavati?

- Do you think she was rude to speak to her father in the way she did?

- Do you think the king was right to throw her out of the palace? If not, why not?

- What sort of life did the king think he was sending his daughter to?

- Why didn't Mairavati give in to the king and do as he asked? Do you think she was brave? What things do you feel strongly about? Could you imagine standing up for those things? What about animal rights, healthy meals at school, or bullying?

❑ Let the children make a montage of pictures from magazines, papers and comics or photos from home. Explain that the montage should represent who they are. It should include things they like and things that they don't like. The size of the pictures and the way they are cut out can show how they feel about different subjects, for example by cutting some out with jagged edges, using borders, or adding words. The idea is for someone else to be able to look at the picture and learn a little about the person it represents.

❑ Let the children play the game of Consequences in groups. This is a fun way to introduce the idea that all our actions have consequences, and sometimes things need to be thought through before they are acted on. Give each child a copy of Activity sheet 1 (page 64). They begin by writing down a girl's name (someone they know or a fictional character) and then fold down the paper to cover the name. They pass the pieces of paper to the person on their left. On it they write a boy's name, then pass the folded paper to the left. Continue until all the sections are filled in. Pass the paper one last time and ask everyone to read out what is on the paper they are holding.

❑ Ask the children to write about the characters of the king and his daughter. Ask them to think about whether they like and respect Mairavati, and whether they think that they could stand up for what they believe in such a brave way. Encourage them to use dictionaries and thesauruses to find suitable adjectives.

## Extension

❑ The children could try making a picture for a friend or family member, then asking that person if they think the picture represents them or not. What could be added or taken away?

## Differentiation

❑ Give lower achievers a copy of Activity sheet 2 (page 65). Ask them to look at the words on the sheet. In the story, what did 'strength' mean – physical strength or something else? Ask the children to colour the pictures, then cut out the words to stick next to the appropriate character.

❑ More able children could write about something that they feel passionately about, and what they would be prepared to do to stand up for it.

## Plenary session

❑ Ask the children if they think that there is a way for the king and Mairavati to sort out their differences? How could the king be shown that there are other ways of looking at things, and that Mairavati could have a point? Could Mairavati have got the king to listen to her beliefs without offending or upsetting him?

❑ Ask one child to be the king, another to be Mairavati, and a third to play the queen. The queen's role is to try to mediate and allow both the king and Mairavati to understand the other's point of view. Ask the other children to help with ideas, and swap the role play around as often as is necessary.

❑ Ask the children if any of these techniques could be useful in a playground dispute or at home. Ask the children if they think that it is important to stand up for what we believe.

❑ Ask the children if they think the king would be happy with his decision for the rest of his life. Will he miss his daughter? What about the queen – did he stop to think how she would feel about losing her daughter?

# Mairavati

Mairavati was a little girl born to a king and queen. The queen spent all her days with Mairavati, teaching her right from wrong, teaching her about love and respect, and teaching her the importance of telling the truth. The queen had a pure heart and Mairavati spent her childhood surrounded by kindness and joy. She grew into a beautiful and loving young woman with firm beliefs.

One day Mairavati was with her father, King Ritumardan, in the throne room when some of his trusted courtiers entered. The king enjoyed showing off his finery and his daughter.

"Is she not the most beautiful princess you have ever seen?" he asked the courtiers. They all agreed and Mairavati blushed. The king continued, "And am I not the wealthiest king in the whole world?" Once again the courtiers nodded in agreement.

"But father, you should not boast so. I am sure there are many kingdoms just as wealthy as yours," Mairavati said. Her father felt insulted by this remark and was not at all happy with Mairavati's behaviour.

The courtiers saw the look on his face and at once tried to soothe the king. "There is no doubt that your majesty's kingdom is the most gracious we have ever known," they said.

But this made Mairavati angry. "You do not need to flatter my father," she said. "Surely my father knows his own limitations, and understands that there are other kingdoms just as gracious as his own."

"Daughter! How dare you speak of me like that?" the king shouted in surprise. "Don't you realise that I have the power to make rich men poor and to turn a beggar into a princess if I wish it?" he continued.

But Mairavati softly answered, "Surely, Father, you know that is not true? It is our karma that gives us our fortune, and we must accept our lot in life. Happiness cannot be given nor taken, not by a king or any mortal."

"You insolent girl! You will take back your words. I have the power to make your life happy. If you will not agree with me then I will marry you to the poorest and ugliest man my men can find. Then we shall see how happy you are!" shouted the king.

PHOTOCOPIABLE

Mairavati would not take back what she had said and Ritumardan kept his word. His guards fetched a filthy old leper, found lying in the street, into the palace. With good grace, Mairavati accepted her father's wish and agreed to marry the leper, trusting that her own beliefs would keep her happy.

As soon as Mairavati and the leper were married Ritumardan threw them out of the palace. Mairavati was sent away from her home and all that she had ever known. She would never be able to see her mother again. Even so, she had joy in her heart as she and her husband walked away from the palace. She still believed that her life was the result of karma and accepted her path with grace.

Mairavati's husband begged her to leave him. He told her that he had nothing to offer; surely another man could make her happier? But Mairavati would not leave and she told her husband that she wanted to stay by his side.

"He had no right to make you leave your home and stop you from seeing your mother!" said the leper.

"That's true," she replied. "But nothing my father can do changes how I feel inside. This is my choice. I accept my path."

All of a sudden there was a flash of bright light, and standing before Mairavati there was no longer a leper but a very handsome young man.

"I am King Manichud," he explained, "My home is in Manipur." Mairavati knew as soon as she set eyes on him that this man was pure of heart, a divine being, a god. But she didn't understand what was happening. "I heard about your true spirit and how you always stand up for what you believe. I wanted to test how deep your faith was, so I decided to visit you. I disguised myself as a leper and waited to be found by your father's guards. You have passed my test and proved that a truly happy person, with strong faith, can be happy in any situation, no matter how difficult or how painful."

Manichud took Mairavati's hand and led his queen back to his palace in Manipur where they lived very happily ever after.

# Consequences

Girl's name…

Boy's name…

Place…

Time of day…

She said to him…

He said to her…

They both said…

Finally, the consequence was…

# The king and Mairavati

| loving | deep |
|--------|------|

| true | pompous | angry |
|------|---------|-------|
| strong | selfish | kind |
| narrow-minded | boastful | happy |

# CHAPTER 11

# Love and stories – Judaism

T E A C H E R S '   N O T E S

This chapter is based on a Jewish story, 'The greatest gift of all'. The activities could run over one or two sessions, or be used at other times for social skills training.

## Themes

Love, children, understanding, communication

## Citizenship Scheme of Work

Unit 1 – Taking part; developing skills of communication and participation

## Aims

• To learn to understand how others feel by reading body language and using listening skills.
• To learn to accurately retell a story.
• To understand that there are many different ways of communicating.

## Resources

• The story on page 68
• The photocopiable sheets on pages 70 and 71

## About this religion

Succoth is a Jewish harvest festival and takes place in September/October, lasting seven days. It dates back to when the Jews had to wander the wilderness, homeless. A succah is an open living space, and today the old traditions are still kept when families build sukkot (plural for succah) for the festival. The Jewish religion is taught through a book known as the Torah, which is thought of as a language of love and a way of saying 'Yes' to God. It is claimed to be for all people and teaches us to love our neighbour.

## Whole class starter

❑ Discuss with the class how they are feeling today. Explain that we do not always need words to understand how someone is feeling. Demonstrate by making 'sad', 'happy' and 'angry' faces.

❑ Ask the children to react to each of the situations shown on page 70. How would they walk if they were going to the dentist? How would they feel if they were going to a sleepover? Ask for a volunteer to come to the front of the class. Give them one of the cards and ask them to show without words how they feel about what is on the card. Next ask the class to try and guess how they are feeling and what is on the card.

❑ Then ask the children if they can imagine how their parents felt when they were born, or the first time they were brought home. Can they think of a gift that they still have that was given to them as a baby?

❑ Explain that the story they will hear is about a father who desperately wants to give his new baby a gift to show her how he feels.

❑ Now read the story.

## Activities

• How did Joseph feel about being a father?

• Why did Joseph keep changing his mind about the present? Imagine that you were one of the shopkeepers. What advice could you give Joseph? What gift would you want him to buy?

- Do you think he made a good decision in the end?

❑ Explain to the children that we communicate a lot of what we want another person to know through body language. Explain that you are going to try an activity called Chinese mimes – it is a little like Chinese whispers but uses actions instead of words. Organise the class into groups. Ask one group to come to the front and give the first person in that group one of the cards from page 71. The child mimes the action described on the card to the second person in the group, while the other group members turn their backs. The second person repeats the mime to the third, and so on. The last child tries to guess what the action is. It is interesting to see if the final mime bears any resemblance to the first mime. If the last child can't guess the action, ask the rest of the class (who have seen all the mimes from the beginning) if they can guess correctly.

❑ Ask the children to retell the story about Joseph in the form of a comic strip. Explain that the aim is to include as much detail from the story as possible and to get the information in the right order, which could be quite difficult as there are so many shopkeepers. Give them a time limit of about ten minutes. When the time is up tell the class to stop working. Retell the important points of the story and ask the children how many of the details they have managed to include. Have they told them in the right order?

## Differentiation

❑ More able children could write a sentence for each picture in their comic strip. Less able children could just picture each of the shops in the right order, or the gift from the shop.

## Plenary session

❑ Discuss what happened to the actions of each person as the mime travelled down the line. How observant were the groups? What details did they leave out?

❑ Ask the children how we communicate. Is it only through words? Ask them to think of as many different ways of communicating as they can. Remind them of things like singing, dance and clothing. Suggest that the school uniform 'tells' people which school they are from without using any words or body language. Explain that all our senses can be used to communicate. When they have finished the list, ask for a suggestion from each group and find out if any group has thought of something unusual not picked by others.

❑ End with a game. Put one child in the 'hot spot' at the front of the class. Tell them that they are not allowed to say 'yes' or 'no', and must use other words to answer questions. Then, one at a time, the other children ask simple questions that need a 'yes' or 'no' answer, for example:
Q Is your name Sam?
A It is.
Q Do you like football?
A Sometimes!

# The greatest gift of all

Joseph's heart melted as he looked at his newborn baby girl. Her blue eyes sparkled back at him and his face lit up with pride. "I must get her a gift to show her how special she is to me. But what could I possibly get that would come close to equalling her importance?"

Joseph rushed around desperately trying to think of an idea. "I will go to the toy maker and ask him for the brightest and most beautiful toy he has." So Joseph left his home and made his way to town.

"Mr Toymaker! I want to buy this brightly coloured wooden spinning top. It caught my eye as soon as I walked into the shop. Is it not the best present I could give my precious baby girl?"

"Of course, sir. It is as colourful as the bright clothes we wear at the festivals, which bring joy to us all."

"Clothes for a festival?" said Joseph, now doubting the spinning top. "How beautiful she would look in new clothes, just like a princess. That would be the perfect present."

So Joseph rushed to the tailor. He chose an outfit of silk, embroidered with gold braid. "This must be the best possible gift," he said to the tailor as he was about to pay.

"Yes, sir. It is very fine, and will keep her as warm as freshly baked Sabbath bread."

With that Joseph dropped the clothes and hurried to the baker. As he picked up a specially baked loaf of the best bread, Joseph still had doubts and the baker made the mistake of uttering the words, "A freshly baked loaf keeps you just as warm inside as a young spring lamb in its fleece."

Without a word, Joseph dropped the bread, much to the baker's dismay. The baker followed him to the door and watched as Joseph rushed to the hill where the shepherd was tending his flock.

By this time there was quite a crowd following, watching as this poor confused new father tried to make up his mind.

"This little lamb would make a perfect gift!" said the shepherd. "She's as good as gold."

No sooner had the shepherd mentioned gold than Joseph handed back the bleating lamb and headed for the jeweller.

From the jeweller's shop he was seen heading for the chemist.

The baker shouted to the bemused jeweller, "What did you say to him?"

"I told him that his gold bangle was as precious as the scent of early morning flowers, still shining with dew," replied the jeweller.

At this the baker, tailor and toy maker nodded and watched eagerly for Joseph to emerge from the chemist – but with or without the perfume?

Just as they had suspected, Joseph ran from the chemist empty handed. The poor chemist followed

PHOTOCOPIABLE

Joseph to the door, holding an exquisite bottle of perfume.

"But what did I say?" the chemist shouted to the others.

"He's a new father!" answered the shepherd, "and as he is now entering the fowler's house I guess you mentioned birds?"

"Well now I come to think of it, yes I did. I told him that the perfume he had chosen was as rare as the dove of peace!" replied the chemist.

"That'll be it!" answered the other men.

And sure enough Joseph walked out of the fowler's house with a cage in his hand containing a tiny white dove. Joseph looked quite out of breath.

"Is this it?" he pleaded. "Is this the most perfect gift that I could give my daughter, who is the most precious thing in my life?" The dove cooed.

"Of course it is, Joseph," said the fowler. "The dove's pure white feathers are like the fringes on a prayer shawl, bearing witness to belief in God and hopes for peace. Like the first kiss to a new love, symbolising love and respect and hope for the future."

Joseph stood for a moment in silence. He looked at the men around him. The toymaker, the tailor, the baker, the shepherd and the jeweller and the chemist and fowler.

"Thank you!" he said, and then his face broke into a grin and he stopped looking worried and confused.

"Follow me!" he shouted, and ran back to his home, with all the men following behind.

Joseph ran inside to where his beautiful daughter was sleeping.

"I've searched…" Joseph began.

"Shush!" whispered his wife. "Can't you see, she's asleep?" she said.

"Sorry!" started Joseph. "It's just that I am so happy. I have been all over town to try and find the perfect gift for our daughter, but I had already given it to her, from the moment I first looked at her in your arms."

And Joseph bent down and gently kissed her forehead. The baby woke up.

"Now look what you've done!" said Joseph's wife, but she was smiling. And instead of crying the baby looked lovingly into her father's eyes.

"My gift was love. No one can be truly happy without love. And with love she will have the strength to bear suffering or deal with disappointment and sadness. Love will stop her becoming bitter or turning to hatred. If you give love you receive love."

And Joseph picked up his daughter and gently kissed her dimpled cheek.

# Situations

**Name** _____

# Chinese mimes

Walk into a chemist's shop.

Pick up different bottles of perfume.

Spray some on your wrist.

Sniff it.

Make a face to show it smells horrible!

---

Walk along a path.

Stop to look at flowers.

Pick a flower.

Be stung on the nose by a wasp!

---

Start off lying in bed.

Wake up.

Go to the bathroom.

Brush your teeth.

Go back to your bedroom.

Open the curtain and see snow outside!

# Rights and responsibilities – Judaism

This chapter explores the Jewish story of 'Moses in the bullrushes', from the Old Testament and looks at it from the perspective of human rights. It would work well along side the story of Mairavati (see Chapter 10).

## Themes

Prejudice, challenging unacceptable behaviour, succeeding against all odds

## Citizenship Scheme of Work

Unit 7 – Children's rights; human rights

## Aims

- To begin to understand the idea of universal human rights, and that we all have a responsibility to uphold those rights.
- To understand that all children have the same rights no matter what their race or religion.
- To see how actions affect others and that it is right to try and challenge unacceptable behaviour in others.

## Resources

- The story on page 74
- The photocopiable sheets on pages 76 and 77

## About this religion

The Jews are descended from Israel and were enslaved in Egypt. In this story we discover that Moses is taken into a royal Egyptian family. It is ironic, then, that he goes on to lead the Jews out of slavery into Israel. Moses spoke with God on Mt Sinai, where he received the Torah which included the Ten Commandments. He was 120 when he died!

## Whole class starter

- ❑ Begin by dividing the class into two groups. Organise them by an arbitrary distinction, such as their hair colour or eye colour.
- ❑ Tell the groups that you are going to give them all a quiz, but that each group will be given different questions.
- ❑ Let the first group sit on chairs, and give them very easy questions like: "What is the day today?"; "What is 2 + 2?"; "Spell 'cat'."
- ❑ Then test the second group. Tell the group they have to stand. Ask them very difficult questions like: "What happened at 2pm last Thursday?"; "What is 3462 + 2113 – 5000?"; "Spell 'prefabrication'"; and so on. Some children may get a little upset, and other children may refuse to be treated so unfairly. If either of these situations arises, make sure you explain that the activity is an experiment. Allow discussion and congratulate the children for wanting to stick up for their rights.
- ❑ At the end of the exercise ask the children how they felt. Did they think the experiment was fair? If not, why not? Do they believe that the whole class was treated equally? What was wrong with the testing?
- ❑ Tell them that the story they are about to hear is a Jewish story and at the time of the story the Jews were slaves, which meant that they were treated unfairly and were not seen as equal to others.
- ❑ Now read the story.

## Activities

❑ Ask the children the following questions.

• Why did the Jewish mother hide her baby in the bullrushes? Do you think that it was an easy decision to make?

• What do you think might have happened to the mother if she had tried to fight for her baby's life?

• What do you think it would have been like to be a slave? What would everyday life have been like? Could slaves eat when they wanted? Could they go away on holiday?

❑ Ask the children what they think someone should do if they think they are being treated unfairly. Speak to someone about it? Do nothing and keep quiet? Be unfair back? Discuss each of these options. With the first option, ask the children who they think they should speak to. It could be a friend, a family member, a teacher or another adult. Suggest that if they are uncomfortable talking to someone they know, there are many telephone help lines around to help people in need. Ask if they know about Childline.

❑ Ask the children to consider what they would do if they saw someone bullying another child. Do they think they should just ignore it? Ask if they think there any benefits in being nasty back to the bully. How would they ultimately feel about themselves if they were nasty? Would this stop the unfairness happening to somebody else?

❑ Organise the children into groups. Give each group copies of the pictures of bullying incidents from Activity sheet 1 (page 76, made into cards) and ask them to talk about the incidents in their groups. Ask them to come up with a solution for each card.

## Extension

❑ Ask the children what might have happened to Moses if he had been allowed to live as a slave. On the board write two headings: 'A day in the life of Moses as a slave' and 'A day in the life of Moses as a prince'. Ask the children to think about how the days would differ. Take the class through each character's day. Ask what they might have done before breakfast, what they might eat for breakfast, and go right through the day till bedtime. Compare the two days.

❑ Ask the children to write a diary entry for one of the characters.

## Differentiation

❑ More able children could write a week's worth of diary entries, covering a special event such as a birthday or festival.

❑ Lower achievers could record the information on a tape recorder.

## Plenary session

❑ Ask the children to explain why they think making people slaves is wrong. What makes people the same? What makes us different? Do these differences mean that we have different rights as individuals, or do children all over the world deserve to be treated the same?

❑ Explain to the children that there is a Children's Bill of Rights. Ask the children what they think should be on it. Read some of it out to them. See page 77.

❑ Discuss physical, educational and emotional needs with the children. Then ask them to write up their own bill of rights. Finally compare this list with the United Nations Bill of Children's Rights.

# Moses in the bullrushes

It was a dark and fearful time for the Israelites (also known as Jews, because their religion is Judaism) who lived in Egypt. They were forced to be slaves and had no choice in how they lived their lives.

The Jewish children could not play or learn as the Egyptian children did. They saw the others living a totally different life, with the right to choose where they went, what they ate and who they played with. All over Egypt you would see young Jewish girl slaves working hard.

But if you looked carefully, you would soon notice that there were no slave boys!

This was because the Pharaoh, who was king of Egypt, had ordered that every baby boy born to a Jewish family must be killed at birth. He had done this because he was afraid that there were now so many Jews living in Egypt they would take over his land. This was a terrifying thought for a mother when she discovered that she was going to have a baby – a time which should bring joy to a family, not sorrow. Each Jewish mother would spend her time praying for a little girl. The child would not be free to make choices in her life but at least she would be alive.

One cold bleak night, a baby was born. The mother hid herself away, trying desperately to muffle the cries of her new born baby. The mother had a little boy and she loved him the moment she held him. The thought that he would be torn from her arms and taken to his death was more than she could bear. Tears streamed down her face and onto the soft cheeks of the innocent baby lying next to her heart.

The mother fretted, hour after hour, wondering what she could do to save the life of her child. First she thought she would tell everyone he was a girl, but she soon realised that it would not take long for the Pharaoh's men to find out the truth.

Eventually she made an incredible decision. She looked around the room where they lay. Up on the shelf she spotted a basket, full of dusty old bits and bobs. The mother wrapped her baby in sheets and blankets for warmth and hid him beneath her cloak, then stole out onto the dark streets carrying the basket that would become the baby's cradle. Quietly and secretly she headed away from the town, towards the river.

Once at the side of the river she stopped. She kissed her baby gently on the forehead and placed him in the basket, then she hid the basket amongst the bullrushes.

"May God go with you, my beautiful boy. I trust that he will protect you and that he will send you an Egyptian mother who can love you safely. My love will be with you always."

Then with tears streaming down her face she tried to muffle her painful and bitter cries as she left him, never looking back.

Not long after sunrise the Pharaoh's daughter was taking her morning walk by the river in the golden early morning sun. She saw the basket from the path and curiosity got the better of her. As soon as she set eyes upon the little boy her heart went out to him. At once she decided to raise the child as her own. His name would be Moses. The little Jewish slave boy who had been destined to be killed would instead be brought up as a prince.

# Bullying

Name _____

# Children's rights

These are some of the rights listed in the United Nations Convention on the Rights of the Child.

**Article 9**    You have the right to live with your parents, unless it is bad for you.

**Article 10**    If you and your parents are living in separate countries, you have the right to get back together and live in the same place.

**Article 11**    You should not be kidnapped.

**Article 12**    You have the right to an opinion and for it to be listened to and taken seriously.

**Article 13**    You have the right to find out things and say what you think, through making art, speaking and writing, unless it breaks the rights of others.

**Article 14**    You have the right to think what you like and be whatever religion you want to be, with your parents' guidance.

**Article 15**    You have the right to be with friends and join or set up clubs, unless this breaks the rights of others.

**Article 16**    You have the right to a private life. For instance, you can keep a diary that other people are not allowed to see.

**Article 19**    You have the right to be protected from being hurt or badly treated.

**Article 27**    You have the right to a good enough standard of living. This means you should have food, clothes and a place to live.

**Article 28**    You have the right to education.

# CHAPTER 13

# Our world – Native American

This chapter looks at the Native American story, 'The wind, the rain and the sparrow'. It could be told alongside the story of 'Siddhartha and the swan' (Chapter 3), another story which is concerned with compassion for animals.

## Themes

Balance, weather, interference, protecting the world around us

## Citizenship Scheme of Work

Unit 3 – Animals and us

## Aims

- To identify the basic needs of humans and animals.
- To understand that we can help animals and ourselves by protecting and looking after the environment.
- To recognise how important the weather is.

## Resources

- The story on page 80
- The photocopiable sheets on pages 82 and 83

## About this religion

Story telling is a large part of Native American history, as tales were handed down from generation to generation and not recorded anywhere. They believe in the rhythm and spirit of nature, and live in harmony with the world around them, unlike the Europeans who entered America and saw nature as an obstacle that had to be overcome.

## Whole class starter

❑ Ask the children to list as many different British animals as they can think of, including birds, insects and spiders. Which of those animals have they actually seen in the wild (not on television)? Which might they see around school?

❑ Explain that there used to be a number of other wild animals in Britain, including bears and wolves. Why do they think there are no more bears and wolves? Show the class a picture of a sparrow. Explain that it used to be a very common sight in towns, but lately numbers have dropped. Can they think of any reasons why this might have happened? Suggest ideas like growing numbers of cats, fewer habitats and fewer insects for them to eat.

❑ Ask the children if they have heard of the extinct dodo. Name some animals that are on the endangered list today, such as the gorilla, white rhino and tiger. Ask if any of the children know why animals become extinct. Sometimes, as with the dinosaurs, it is beyond anyone's control, but more often today the problem is the way human beings are behaving on the planet. For example, people cut down trees in the rainforests and animals lose their homes.

❑ Organise the children into groups and give them copies of Activity sheet 1 (page 82). Ask them to cut out the words and put them in order of priority for staying alive. Within the groups opinions will differ, so come together at the end to discuss findings.

- ❑ Tell the children that you are going to read them a story told by Native American people. Explain that in Native American culture people show a lot of respect for the planet, believing that we only share the Earth with other living things and that it is not ours to do as we please with.

- ❑ Now read the story.

## Activities

- ❑ Ask the children the following questions.

- Why did the villagers want to get rid of the wind and the rain? Have you ever wished that they would go away? Are there ways that you could make a rainy or very windy day better? (Splashing in puddles, flying a kite or playing indoor games.)

- Could we live without the rain?

- Did the villagers stop to think about the consequences of what they asked for?

- ❑ Ask the children to make a list of pros and cons for the different aspects of the weather. Give them examples such as: "Sun – makes plants grow, gives you sunburn,"; "Rain – fills up the lakes, can cause floods,"; "Wind – helps spread seeds, can damage houses."

- ❑ Set up an experiment to find out the best conditions for growth using plants with vigorous seedlings, such as beans or sunflowers. Give some plants too much water, some no water and some just the right amount. In different pots do the same with light and air. You could tell the class that some people believe talking to plants makes them grow bigger because they like to feel the breath on their leaves and they enjoy the extra carbon dioxide!

- ❑ Ask the children what they think animals need for survival. Discuss their needs at different times of the year. Using the recording sheet on Activity sheet 2 (page 83), set up an animal count. Choose an area of the school grounds that can be adapted for this activity and ask the class to take it in turns to count the animals that they see

there throughout a certain period of time. Discuss everyone's findings. Ask if the count changed at certain times of day and ask them to think about things that might be affecting whether the animals such as birds come to the area or not. Mention things like playtime, traffic and local cats.

- ❑ Make a spider chart showing jobs done by the weather, for example the sun warming a beach, rain filling a pond where someone is fishing or a windmill grinding wheat. Let the children draw pictures of the weather jobs, describe them in words, or do both.

## Differentiation

- ❑ More able children could write an explanation of the job that the weather is doing.

- ❑ Less able children could just do the pictures, while still creating the recording sheets.

## Plenary session

- ❑ Ask the class what the children in the story enjoyed about the wind and the rain. What did the sparrow teach the people of the village when they realised that food was harder to grow and the river was disappearing?

- ❑ Reconsider the area where birds visit at school. Ask the children if any of them have made a bird-friendly area at home. Do they think that more birds now attend the area? Do a plan for a bird-friendly area at school. (Later you can do a count in the school bird area to see if more birds visit since the changes were made.)

- ❑ Look again at the seedlings that were grown. Which have survived, flourished or died?

- ❑ Finally, ask the children to draw conclusions from their activities. How important is the weather to our environment? How important is the environment to the animals around us? Are there things that we can do to help?

# The wind, the rain and the sparrow

"Hey, this is a great game!" said the wind, watching the children laugh as they chased the feather he was blowing away. Meanwhile the rain was making muddy puddles – perfect for splashing through or making mud pies. Then a voice was heard calling the children. It was time for their lessons.

The wind and the rain were left alone to find something to do, but there was not much that was as fun as playing with the children.

"Watch me!" shouted the wind suddenly as he blew through a tent, tearing away an animal skin from the wall. This was a great new game.

"Bet you can't get in there!" he teased his friend.

"Oh can't I? Watch!" called the rain, who did his best to batter his way through the deer skin walls, soaking the rugs within.

Then he said, "I know another great game. Follow me." And the wind and the rain chased to where the fires were burning.

"Can you put out that fire?" asked the rain.

"Of course I can," said the wind. He blew and blew, but instead of putting the fire out, he just seemed to make the flames bigger. The flames scorched the meat that was cooking for lunch and turned it black.

"I knew you couldn't do it!" mocked the rain, "Watch me." And he rained as hard as he could onto the fire, leaving nothing but a sludgy mess.

"That was brilliant," said the wind, "Now what shall we do?"

They saw a family just back from fishing and decided that they could play lots of games with them.

The poor family returned to their tent, cold and soaked through by the rain's game. Their clothes were torn and their fish had been blown out of their hands by the wind. The people of the village were becoming more and more angry with the troublesome pair.

A meeting was called and the sun was summoned. The villagers told the sun that they wanted to get rid of the wind and the rain. The village had had enough of their silly games!

"Are you sure this is what you really want?" the sun asked slowly.

"Of course it is," replied the oldest person in the village. "They make such a mess and they ruin our food. We get cold and have to keep repairing our tents. It will be far easier without them."

"Well if you are sure," answered the beaming voice, "I will tell them that they are not wanted!"

And so the wind and the rain left the village. Sadly they wandered far and wide. They didn't understand why they had to leave the home where they had enjoyed their games, but they agreed never to return.

To begin with everyone in the village was happy. They danced; they cooked special feasts using fish from their dry, wind-still fishing trips. The sun shone down just as he always had, beaming brightly, smiling sleepily.

Then one day the villagers saw a different home to the one that they were used to. Where was their green grass? Why was it so tricky to catch a fish? And why did they spend so much time hiding away from their friend the sun?

"You need the breeze of the wind to cool your face!" said a sparrow who had been listening to the people in the village. "And another thing!" he added. "That grass and grain would be much tastier, and there would be a lot more of it, with the help of the rain to refresh it. By the way, didn't there used to be a river where that stream now flows? It's no wonder my mate the salmon has moved down to the sea. His home has nearly disappeared."

The villagers looked at one another and one of the children cried, "I miss the rain and the wind. Why can't they come home?"

"But we were so horrible to them, chasing them away. Why would they ever come back? And where did they go?" said an elder.

"We could give them a present," said another.

"Give them my feather!" said the child, "It might remind them of the fun we used to have."

"But how will we find them?" said the elder.

"I will go for you!" said the sparrow. "Give me the feather and I will fly high and whistle until they answer." So the sparrow took the feather and flew and searched, soaring high up into the clouds singing all the way.

The children watched every day hoping for all three to return. And as they waited the village got weaker. The crops stopped growing and the dust got thicker. The people of the village realised how stupid they had been in sending away the rain and the wind, when all the time the sun kept shining, seeming to grow stronger and stronger. They realised what a terrible mistake they had made and they prayed that the wind and rain would forgive them and come home.

Then one day – "Look," shouted a little voice. "My feather, my feather. It's my feather – they've come back."

The wind was chasing the feather back home and the rain could be heard pattering along behind on the sun-baked ground. The children shouted with delight and the villagers cheered. The sparrow announced their arrival to the whole village, adding, "I think it's party time!"

# Life's needs

Read the words below. Cut them out and put them in the order of priority you think they come for staying alive.

| | | |
|---|---|---|
| children | something to do | television |
| love | safety | food |
| a home | predators | air |
| trees | warmth | friends |
| health | treats | water |

PHOTOCOPIABLE

**Name** ——————————————————————

# Animal watching

| Date and time | Name of animal | Sketch of animal | Comments |
|---|---|---|---|
| | | | |
| | | | |
| | | | |
| | | | |
| | | | |

# What is a community? – Sikhism

This chapter focuses on the Sikh story, 'The emperor and the langar'. The story of 'The river goddess' (Chapter 1) could be told alongside this story, as could the Hindu story 'Prince Prahlad and the demon king' (Chapter 7).

## Themes

Community, duty and social responsibility, doing what you can to help others

## Citizenship Scheme of Work

Unit 5 – Living in a diverse world
Unit 10 – Local democracy for young citizens

## Aims

- To understand the idea of community and begin to realise how a community can help individuals.

## Resources

- The story on page 86
- Materials for making a quilt

## About this religion

The word Sikh means 'a learner' or 'disciple', and Sikhs believe only in one God (Ik Onkar). It is a young religion. The first Guru (Guru Nanak) was born in 1469AD. The Sikh religion believes strongly in communal seva (which means 'selfless service'), and community is very highly valued.

## Whole class starter

❑ Explain to the children that a gurdwara is a place where Sikhs go to pray. After prayer they are all invited to eat in the langar, a kitchen at the gurdwara. The meals are free and open to everyone, not just Sikhs, and the food and service are provided free by people from the local Sikh community.

❑ Now read the story.

## Activities

❑ Ask the children the following questions:

- Do you think Guru Amar Das was right not to celebrate the Emperor's visit? Did he take into consideration all the villagers' opinions?

- Why do you think he decided to treat the Emperor in the same way that he would treat anyone else? (Try to put across the importance of equality in the Sikh religion.)

- Why do you think Guru Amar Das refused Emperor Akbar's offer of land?

❑ Explain to the class that they are going to form three committees to decide how to welcome visitors to the school. Each committee will be given a different type of visitor to welcome: a member of the royal family; prospective parents and their child; and a group of foreign school children. Each committee will elect two of their members to join a council. At the end of the committee's discussion the council members will join together to judge presentations from each of the committees. Give the groups ten to twenty minutes to come up with ideas to present to council. Then ask the council to listen to each presentation and decide whether they agree with the proposal from each group, taking into consideration cost, time and whether the idea is appropriate to the school.

❑ Organise the children into groups and tell them their task is to plan a langar and to decide who would do what. The jobs must be shared out equally, making sure that everyone understands their role and is happy with it. The jobs are: preparing the food, cooking it, laying the tables, serving the people and washing up. When all the groups have made their plans go through them with the whole class. Which jobs were liked and which ones were not? Is everyone happy with the job they have ended up with? You may find that not many children were happy having to do the washing up. Discover whether this problem has been resolved – or did they just avoid allocating the jobs nobody wanted? Try to come up with a way of resolving the problem, for example taking turns to do the washing up.

❑ Tell the children that they are going to make a quilt, each child making a square for it. Say that the quilt needs a theme and suggest 'our faces', 'our hands', 'school colours' and 'togetherness', or take suggestions from the class. They need to discuss what will happen to the quilt once it is made. Perhaps it should go on the wall at school to represent the class and how hard they have worked. Or perhaps they should auction the quilt to raise money for something the class needs, or for charity. Ask for other suggestions.

## Differentiation

❑ Organise the group activities using the children's individual strengths, mixing levels of ability, so that they are encouraged to help each other. Those who write well could do the scribing, those who speak clearly can give presentations, those with good IT skills could research ideas, and so on.

## Plenary session

❑ Ask the children if they understand what a community is. Ask them to explain what the school community is. Explain that *seva* means 'selfless service' and this is the word used in the langar for the people serving the food. What does 'selfless' mean? How does the langar affect the community?

❑ Look back over the class responsibility network. Are people still doing their given jobs? Does having a job or role within the class give people a feeling of importance? Ask the children if they think Guru Amar Das was right to refuse the Emperor's offer of land. Ask the children if they believe human beings need to feel useful.

# The emperor and the langar

The village of Goindwal rested peacefully on the banks of the River Beas. As the water rolled along, time seemed to slow. Guru Amar Das made his way to preach to the people on the river bank. He could always be found there. A lot of the time he would simply sit meditating, with calmness flowing from him like the water that passed gently by.

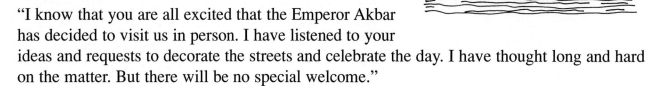

Today though, there was a breeze of excitement as the villagers whispered amongst themselves and waited for instruction.

"I know that you are all excited that the Emperor Akbar has decided to visit us in person. I have listened to your ideas and requests to decorate the streets and celebrate the day. I have thought long and hard on the matter. But there will be no special welcome."

The crowd gasped. Nothing special to celebrate the Emperor coming to their village?

"The Emperor," said Guru Amar Das quietly, "is a great and wise man."

Emperor Akbar was not a Sikh, but a Muslim and one of the things that made him wise was that he had respect for all religions.

"But," continued the Guru "he is also human. Everyone entering our village or eating in the langar should be treated equally, as God would wish it. They must all be treated with kindness and welcomed openly whether emperor or beggar."

So when the Emperor arrived, he was shown straight to the langar. Some of the villagers were scared. Surely they should have put up banners? Surely there should be music and celebrations for the great Akbar, Emperor of India? For those who did not trust in Guru Amar Das and in God it was a fretful time. Some did not want to venture out from their homes, believing that Akbar would be angry and punish them.

At the langar, however, the Emperor observed how everyone behaved and sat on the floor with all the people. He did not expect to be treated differently. He had asked to come to Goindwal to meet Guru Amar Das because he had heard great things about him and had become interested in him and his religion. He wanted to learn more about Sikhs. After all, they were all his people. So he expected no special treatment.

PHOTOCOPIABLE

The Emperor and the villagers ate a simple meal of rice, lentils and bread. Akbar learned the importance of the langar. He appreciated that the food had come from all the people in the village and that they gave it lovingly even when they had very little for themselves. The Emperor was able to see how everyone in this village became a special part of the community by giving to the langar.

When the meal was over the Emperor wanted to do something to help, and offered Guru Amar Das some of his land.

"It is good earth and would grow many crops and feed many people at the langar," he said. But gently, and without offending the Emperor, Guru Amar Das turned down the offer. He said, "It is the responsibility of every individual to give their share to the langar. If you take this from them you also take a little of their pride and lessen their strong sense of community."

All this made sense to Emperor Akbar, and he felt that he had a lot to take away with him from his visit to Goindwal. Guru Amar Das made his way back to the banks of the river and returned to his prayers and meditation.

# CHAPTER 15

# Want versus need – Sikhism

Duni Chand is obsessed with possessions and material gain. He sees his status as being defined by how much money he has. Guru Nanak, the first guru, wants to show him that becoming one with God will only be achieved by good deeds and actions and not thinking about oneself but by helping others. The story links to Units 2 and 5 from the Citizenship Scheme Of Work and would work well alongside the Muslim story of Ali's Hajj (see Chapter 8).

## Themes

Equality, needs and wants, spirituality and the Sikh religion

## Citizenship Scheme of Work

Unit 5 – Living in a diverse world
Unit 11 – In the media – what's the news?

## Aims

- To consider the differences between need and want.
- To consider how helping others might affect our own lives in a good way.
- To think about status and equality within a community, and learn about the Sikh perspective of all being equal.

## Resources

- The story on page 90
- The photocopiable sheets on pages 92 and 93

## About this religion

Guru Nanak, the first guru, believed that the true God would not require ritual and doctrinal controversies, as is seen with some other religion but was concerned with truth and equality; at the same time he never believed other religions to be worthless or untrue. The Sikhs share some of the Hindu festivals, but worship tends to be a lot simpler in comparison.

## Whole class starter

❑ Tell the children that in the story they are about to hear the character of Duni Chand believes himself to be more important than lots of other people.

❑ Before reading the story give the children a copy of Activity sheet 1 (page 92) and ask them to cut out the names and pictures and put them in order of priority. Who do they think is the most important?

❑ Discuss their answers and then ask who they would offer to help first if there was an accident, and why. What makes one person more important than another, if anything?

❑ Then read the story.

### Questions

❑ Ask the children the following:

- Why did Guru Nanak ask Duni Chand to carry the needle for him?

- The word 'guru' means teacher. What was the Guru trying to teach Duni Chand?

- Why did Guru Nanak not want to go to the dinner party with Duni Chand?

## Activities

❑ Brainstorm ideas for a party. This should include things such as food, decoration and entertainment. Discuss how much this would cost. The organise the class into groups and ask them, instead of a party for themselves, to come up with an idea that would help others, using the same amount of money. (The ideas could include a party for senior citizens or giving the money to charity.)

❑ Tell the children to imagine they were going to a deserted island and can only take three things with them. Which things would they choose to take? Would they take things that were useful or things that made them feel happy, like a favourite toy? Suggest three things that you might take and explain why.

❑ List all the things suggested on the board. Discuss which are wanted or needed. Talk about the difference between wanting and needing. Try to find out if the children can differentiate between emotional or spiritual need and physical need. Ask if they can survive without their emotional needs – if so what sort of life would that be? What sort of life would you choose, a material life or a spiritual life?

❑ Give each child a copy of Activity sheet 2 (page 93). Read through the facts. Ask the children to draw their own picture of Guru Nanak and then label the picture with at least three of the facts about Sikhs and Guru Nanak. Ask them to choose the facts which they think are the most important, rather than just copy them all down.

Additional information on the Sikh religion that might be of use:

• Sikhs believe in one god.

• Sikh means 'learner' or disciple.

• Guru Nanak was the first guru (b1469AD). There were nine more.

• After the tenth guru died, the Sikh scriptures were written down. These have become known as Guru Granth Sahib and are shown the same respect as a human guru, as all the spiritual teachings are kept in this book.

• Sikhism is Britain's third most popular religion.

• Sikhs believe that religion should be practised by living and coping with everyday problems.

• Sikhs believe in social and sexual equality.

• Sikhs believe that to become one with God they must work hard and live honestly.

• Sikhs must serve others and switch their attention from self to God.

## Differentiation

❑ More able children can write a list of reasons why boys and girls are or are not equal.

❑ Less able children could use a tick sheet to discover if girls and boys are equal. (For example, equal in strength – yes/no; equal in running – yes/no; equal in listening skills–; equal in cooking abilities–.)

## Extension

❑ Ask a member of the Sikh community to come and talk to the class.

## Plenary session

❑ Looking back at the story, ask the children why Guru Nanak gave Duni Chand the needle, and why the Guru was pleased to see Duni Chand when he came to ask about the task. The story says that in the end Duni Chand was happier because he gave to others and helped those in need. Ask the children to explain why this was.

❑ Ask the class to write about why it is good to help others. They could use these sentence openings:
"When I help my friend I feel…"
"Watching someone open the present I gave them makes me feel…"
"When I see another person in pain I want to…"
"Watching children from poor countries on television makes me feel…"

# Duni Chand and the needle

While you sit and listen to this story, I want you to look around. I bet the room is full of interesting things, and I bet you get excited when there is something new.

Do you get bored with games from last year? Are you always wanting more things? There are 'things' everywhere!

Now, close your eyes. Go on – you don't need anything except your ears to listen to a story! With your eyes closed you can make a story even better.

Imagine a fire-breathing dragon, with shark-like teeth. Careful now, keep quiet! He breathes multicoloured fire and he sounds like a rattling, boiling old kettle as he breathes.

He's coming closer… be careful. Oh, no! Look out, he's… (No, don't open your eyes.)

…He's really angry. He's creeping up behind your teacher, getting closer…

OK, who opened their eyes? Now we'll never know what happened next!

Unless of course you can retell the story yourselves. You won't need a thing to do it!

**************************

The story I'm going to tell you now is to help you think about whether the 'things' in it are important or not.

A long time ago there was a very wealthy banker named Duni Chand. He would take every opportunity to show off his jewels, his new belongings and the expensive gifts he bought for his wife. He was always boasting to his friends and colleagues: "I have so much. I must be the most successful man who has ever lived!"

One day Guru Nanak, the first Sikh, came to the city of Lahore where Duni Chand lived. Of course, Duni Chand never missed an opportunity to show off, and went to find Guru Nanak. He begged him to come for a special feast in his honour. Guru Nanak politely refused but the banker tried again and again. Guru Nanak replied that he preferred the simpler things in life and was not interested in feasts and celebrations. This made no sense at all to Duni Chand. "Who wouldn't want to come to a feast put on specially for them?" he wondered. He sent more and more invitations until in the end it was impossible for Guru Nanak to refuse to come to the feast.

After a truly fabulous meal, Duni Chand felt very grand indeed, with everyone telling him what a marvellous occasion it was. He then turned to Guru Nanak and said, "You must know that I am a very wealthy man here in Lahore. Just look at my magnificent home and belongings. If ever there is anything that I can do for you, please just ask."

Guru Nanak thought for a while as he watched the guests dressed in their finery drooling over Duni Chand's gold and silver.

"It is true," he thought, "so much treasure. Soon there will be nowhere to sit!"

And then a smile came to his face and he said, "There is one thing you could do for me."

"Anything!" replied Duni Chand.

"Take this fine silver needle and keep it safe for me until we meet in the next world."

"Oh! Guru Nanak must think me so important," he said to his wife later that evening.

"Really?" said his wife, as she cleared away the plates.

"Stop doing that!" said her husband, annoyed that she showed so little interest. "You must listen and look."

He held out the silver needle with the pride of a lion and explained Guru Nanak's instructions. But Duni Chand didn't quite get the response he was expecting.

"I think you'd better go and find the Guru before he leaves," she laughed "and find out how you can do as he asks." And with that she giggled her way off to bed, leaving her puzzled husband behind her.

At first light Duni Chand went in search of Guru Nanak and an explanation. When he found him he said, "Please, your Holiness! How can I do as you ask? It isn't a problem for me to take care of your needle, indeed it's an honour. But how can I take it with me into heaven?"

Guru Nanak was pleased to see Duni Chand. He had hoped to see him again.

"Duni Chand," he began, "is the needle not very small? Tiny, in fact and light, as a feather?"

Duni Chand nodded his head. "Then if you do not know a way of taking this tiny needle into heaven, how will you take all your belongings, your silver and gold, all the things that you believe are so important? What will you do with your magnificent home and wealth?"

Duni Chand sat down. His eyes fell to the ground as he began to understand all that Guru Nanak was saying. He felt ashamed as he realised the extent of his greed, and saw how pompous he must look to others! His riches and wealth were worth nothing – he could take none of them with him into heaven when he died!

Duni Chand was lucky to have met Guru Nanak, and to have learned the lesson offered to him by the great man. He realised that all his wealth had never actually made him happy. By following Nanak's teachings he found a deeper love of God, one he had never known before. From that day forward Duni Chand gave money away to the poor and food to the hungry. He would always help anyone in need and by doing these things he found true happiness – giving 'things' away, not collecting them!

**Name** _____

# Who is important?

Queen

Builder

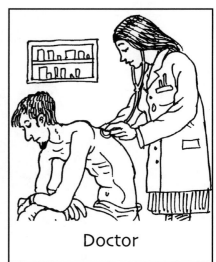

Doctor

Cleaner

Cook

Road sweeper

Judge

Rich person

Poor person

# The Sikh religion

## Guru Nanak

The word 'Sikh' means 'someone who learns'

'Sewa' means 'helping others'. Sikhs believe that helping others brings them closer to God.

Guru Nanak was the first guru of the Sikh faith.

At the age of 30 Guru Nanak disappeared for three days. On his return he said that God had spoken to him in a vision.

He said that the way to live was to be truthful and treat everyone as equal. God had told him to teach this to others.

Other famous gurus are Guru Amar Das and Guru Gobind Singh.

# Useful websites

*Citizenship*
www.standards.dfes.gov.uk/schemes2/ks1-2citizenship
Gives full details on Citizenship units at Key Stages 1 and 2.

*All religions*
www.bbc.co.uk/religion/religions

Extremely informative and well organised site giving details of history, customs, beliefs, worship, holy days and features of fourteen different religions (including atheism).

www.ers.north-ayrshire.gov.uk/topics.htm
This page gives links to all the North Ayrshire topics pages, including pages of links to resources on each of the major religions. Each page is divided up into General, Festivals, Stories, Traditions and Resources (books). These are all subdivided into pages suitable for either pupils or teachers/parents. Asterisks indicate interactive pages.

www.teachingreligion.com/index.html
Useful US website providing information on many religions to school teachers. It also discusses issues of teaching religion and offers classroom activities.

*Buddhism*
www.dharmaforkids.com

A user-friendly site with well organised information on many aspects of Buddhism. Includes stories from the Buddha's life, art gallery, activities, teachers' notes and an interactive nun (click on her image on the home page to see more).

www.fwbo.org
The official site of the Friends of the Western Buddhist Order. Not aimed at children, but clear and well organised.

*Christianity*
www.request.org.uk

Well designed and balanced site with sections for infants, KS2 and above, and teachers (including a 'Teacher's Guide to Using the Internet in Religious Education')

www.topmarks.co.uk/religious/default.aspx

Illustrated interactive versions of the stories of the birth of Jesus and Easter (also Moses and Joseph).

*Hinduism*
www.btinternet.com/~vivekananda/schools1.htm

A helpful and informative site on many aspects of Hinduism. The 'Key Stage 1' pages appear to be for all primary (but more suitable for KS2); the 'Key Stage 2 and 3' pages are actually for secondary. The links page has links to stories and to a site featuring 'virtual poojas' – Hindu worship in interactive cyber form (www.eprarthana.com/virtual/vpooja.asp). Choose your Hindu god. Best with speakers on in order to hear the mantras.

www.hindu.org
Comprehensive site with section for teachers.

*Islam*
www.islam-guide.com/contents-wide.htm
Information on Islam from a believer's viewpoint. Presents a scientific case for the truth of the Qur'an.

*Jainism*
www.jainworld.com/index.asp

Very comprehensive site giving information on Jainism: history, philosophy, educational materials. The 'Educational materials' section contains a sub-section with 32 Jain stories, including a version of 'King Hansa'.

The literature section includes
www.jainworld.org/general/prem/Cartoons/cartoon.htm

which tells the story of Bhagwan Rishabhdev in comic format.

*Judaism*
www.twocandles.com

Jewish songs for and by children.

www.topmarks.co.uk/religious/default.aspx
Illustrated interactive versions of the stories of Moses and Joseph (also Jesus and Easter). Moses story links to a good page on the Ten Commandments, with an activity page.

*Native American (Navajo)*
http://navajo-indian.org

Starting point for information on all aspects of Navajo life.

www.bedtime-story.com/bedtime-story/navajo-rainbow.htm
Child-friendly version of the birth story of the twins Monster-Slayer and Born-of-Water.

www.ewebtribe.com/NACulture/stories.htm
Links to Native American legends and stories.

*Sikhism*
www.sikhnet.com

An interesting and wide ranging site primarily aimed at Sikhs but of interest to anyone who wants to find out about this religion. The 'SikhiWiki' is an encyclopedia of Sikhism, including an excellent introduction to the religion. The 'Sikh Youth' section contains a collection of illustrated stories (www.sikhnet.com/s/SikhStories). The Gurbani section (www.sikhnet.com/Gurbani) has a large selection of audio files of music and stories. (You will need Real Player to listen.)

*Sufism*
www.windsofchange.net/archives/cat_features_sufi_wisdom.php
Sufi wisdom and deceptively simple stories that children will probably be able to read but which they will need to think about.

www.zahuri.org/Sufistories.html
Short Sufi stories, not especially aimed at children but short enough for them to read or for you to adapt.